Cloud-First Strategies

Cloud-First Strategies

The Future of IT Infrastructure in India

REFEAL MECHLORE

Readers Publications

CONTENTS

INDEX

Chapter 5: Hybrid and Multi-Cloud Strategies

5.1 Embracing Hybrid and Multi-Cloud Environments

5.2 Advantages and Challenges of Hybrid Cloud

5.3 Managing Complexity and Ensuring Consistency

Chapter 6: Cloud-Native Technologies and Innovations

6.1 The Role of Cloud-Native Technologies (Containers, Serverless, Microservices)

6.2 Leveraging AI and ML in Cloud Environments

6.3 Edge Computing and Its Impact on Cloud

Chapter 7: Skill Development and Workforce Transformation

7.1 Addressing the Cloud Skills Gap in India

7.2 Training and Upskilling Initiatives

7.3 Building Cloud-Ready Teams

7.4 Collaborations with Educational Institutions

Chapter 8: Overcoming Challenges and Pitfalls

8.1 Common Challenges in Cloud Adoption

8.2 Strategies for Mitigating Risks

8.3 Avoiding Common Pitfalls

8.4 Best Practices for Cloud Governance

Chapter 9: Future Trends and Predictions

9.1 The Evolving Cloud Landscape in India

9.2 Emerging Technologies (Edge Computing, Quantum Computing)

9.3 Regulatory and Legislative Changes

9.4 Preparing for the Future

Chapter 10: Recommendations and Actionable Insights

10.1 Developing a Cloud-First Roadmap

10.2 Building a Business Case for Cloud Adoption

10.3 Steps to Ensure Data Security and Compliance

10.4 Nurturing a Cloud-Centric Culture

INTRODUCTION

In the huge and various scene of India, a computerized change of fantastic extents is unfurling. At the core of this change lies the key and dynamic combination of distributed computing, introducing another time of IT framework. The story of India's computerized development is an exciting story of mechanical advancement, versatility, and the strength of a country that is ready to saddle the tremendous capability of the cloud.

"Cloud-First Procedures: The Eventual fate of IT Foundation in India" is a far reaching investigation of this extraordinary excursion. This book unwinds the many-sided layers of cloud-first methodologies and their urgent job in forming the fate of IT framework in India. It is a story of chance, transformation, and the aggregate endeavors of people, associations, and policymakers to embrace the computerized age.

1. **The Computerized Change Basic in India:**
   The presentation sets the stage by featuring the computerized change basic that India faces. It is an excursion set apart by remarkable development in digitaliza-tion, powered by variables like the far and wide reception of cell phones, the prospering web based business area, and the public authority's aggressive drives like Computerized India. In this specific circumstance, we investigate how India's IT foundation has turned into the bedrock whereupon this advanced change is assembled.

2. **The Ascent of Cloud-First Methodologies:**
   With the comprehension of the computerized scene, we progress to the center idea of cloud-first systems. The expression "cloud-first" addresses an essential change in the IT worldview, stressing the reception of cloud-based arrange-ments as really important over conventional on-premises framework. The presentation explains the meaning of cloud-first methodologies in enhancing the readiness, adaptability, and development capacities of associations in India.

3. **The Complex Advantages of Cloud-First Methodologies:**
   Diving further, we investigate the huge number of advantages that cloud-first

methodologies offer. From engaging associations to scale their tasks productively to upgrading cost-viability and empowering quick advancement, these methodologies alter how organizations and government substances work in India's developing computerized scene. Contextual investigations and genuine models delineate the unmistakable benefits of embracing cloud-first ways of thinking.

4. **Exploring the Cloud Administration and Organization Models:**
As the cloud-first excursion unfurls, it is urgent to comprehend the different cloud administration models (Framework as a Help - IaaS, Stage as a Help - PaaS, Programming as a Help - SaaS) and organization models (public, private, crossover, and multi-cloud). This part gives the essential establishment to arrive at educated conclusions about the right blend regarding administrations and arrangement models custom-made to India's novel requirements.

5. **The Urgent Significance of Cloud Security and Consistence:**
Right after India's computerized development, information protection and security arise as principal concerns. This part jumps into the intricacies of information security in India's administrative scene, tending to difficulties like information restriction and sway. It highlights the basic job of cloud suppliers in offering strong safety efforts and guaranteeing consistence with India's administrative system.

6. **Embracing Mixture and Multi-Cloud Systems:**
Perceiving the developing pattern of associations looking for a fair way to deal with cloud reception, we investigate half breed and multi-cloud techniques. These techniques empower associations to tackle the qualities of various cloud suppliers and sending models, finding some kind of harmony between control, adaptability, and cost-proficiency. True contextual analyses represent the benefits and difficulties of these methodologies.

7. **The Time of Cloud-Local Advancements and Developments:**
The computerized scene in India isn't static; it is consistently developing. In this specific circumstance, we dive into the job of cloud-local advancements, including holders, serverless figuring, and microservices. These advancements, alongside arising patterns like edge registering and the reconciliation of computerized reasoning (simulated intelligence) and AI (ML), are reshaping India's IT framework scene.

8. **Abilities Advancement and Labor force Change:**
The extraordinary excursion to cloud-first systems requires a change in labor force abilities. This segment resolves the major problem of the cloud abilities hole in India and presents a dream for labor force change. Drives, coordinated efforts with instructive organizations, and the significance of constant upskilling become the dominant focal point.

9. **Contextual analyses of Cloud Examples of overcoming adversity in India:** Drawing motivation from true models, this segment features driving associations that have effectively embraced cloud-first procedures. These contextual investigations give important bits of knowledge into the pragmatic use of cloud-first methodologies across different businesses, including medical services, finance, web based business, and that's only the tip of the iceberg.

10. **Beating Difficulties and Traps:** Indeed, even despite groundbreaking open doors, difficulties and entanglements exist. This part explores normal hindrances in cloud reception and offers techniques to alleviate chances. By analyzing best practices and staying away from normal stumbles, associations in India can set out on their cloud-first excursion with certainty.

11. **Looking into What's in store:** What's in store coaxes with commitments of additional advancement and change. In this last part of the presentation, we look forward to the advancing cloud scene in India. We think about arising advances, administrative changes, and the developing job of cloud-first methodologies in quite a while's computerized future.

12. **Proposals and Noteworthy Experiences:**

As a reasonable manual, "Cloud-First Techniques" finishes up by giving proposals and significant bits of knowledge. Perusers will find how to foster a cloud-first guide, fabricate a convincing business case for cloud reception, guarantee information security and consistence, and sustain a cloud-driven culture inside their associations.

1. **The Evolving Landscape of IT Infrastructure**
The scene of IT framework is in a ceaseless condition of change. In the present advanced age, where data and innovation penetrate each feature of our lives, the manner in which we configuration, make due, and use IT framework has never been more basic. This powerful development mirrors the persevering walk of innovative advancement and the always expanding requests of our interconnected world. In this investigation, we dive into the developing scene of IT foundation, figuring out its authentic setting, latest things, and the future it guarantees.

Authentic Setting
To see the value in the advancement of IT framework, we should initially project our look back to its starting points. Many years prior, IT foundation principally contained on-premises servers, centralized computers, and exclusive equipment. These frameworks were housed in committed server farms, frequently described by lines of servers and the steady murmur of cooling hardware.

The client-server model overwhelmed, with associations possessing and keeping up with their equipment and programming stack. This approach considered a serious level of control and security yet was intrinsically resolute and exorbitant to scale. Each new application or administration required the procurement of extra equipment, prompting rambling server farms and underutilized assets. The turn of the 21st century introduced a change in outlook with the ascent of virtualization. Innovations like VMware permitted various virtual machines to run on a solitary actual server, streamlining asset usage and decreasing equipment costs. This obvious the start of a more unique and nimble IT foundation scene.

Latest things

Distributed computing: Distributed computing has arisen as the key part of present day IT framework. It offers the versatility, adaptability, and cost-productivity that conventional on-premises arrangements frequently battle to coordinate. Public cloud suppliers like Amazon Web Administrations (AWS), Microsoft Sky blue, and research Cloud have democratized admittance to cutting edge processing assets, empowering organizations, everything being equal, to enhance and scale quickly.

Virtualization and Containerization: Virtualization advancements, joined with containerization stages like Docker and Kubernetes, have changed how applications are conveyed and made due. They give the nimbleness to make, scale, and move applications flawlessly across various conditions, from on-premises server farms to the cloud.

Edge Registering: The expansion of Web of Things (IoT) gadgets and the requirement for low-inertness handling has led to edge figuring. This approach permits information to be handled nearer to the source, diminishing idleness and empowering ongoing navigation. Edge figuring is reshaping IT foundation by stretching out registering assets to the fringe of organizations.

Programming Characterized Everything: Programming characterized foundation, including Programming Characterized Systems administration (SDN) and Programming Characterized Stockpiling (SDS), abstracts the fundamental equipment, making it more adaptable and programmable. It empowers the powerful distribution of assets and improves on network the board.

Simulated intelligence and Robotization: Man-made brainpower (man-made intelligence) and AI (ML) are progressively being incorporated into IT foundation to upgrade execution, anticipate disappointments, and mechanize routine errands. Computer based intelligence driven experiences are assisting associations with advancing asset usage and work on the general effectiveness of their framework.

Cross breed and Multi-Cloud: Numerous associations are embracing mixture and multi-cloud systems to adjust the advantages of public and confidential cloud conditions. This approach permits them to keep up with command over basic information and applications while utilizing the versatility and development of public mists.

The Eventual fate of IT Foundation

Quantum Processing: Quantum registering holds the commitment of tackling complex issues that are presently past the abilities of traditional PCs. While it is still in its earliest stages, quantum registering can possibly reform fields like cryptography, drug revelation, and advancement.

5G Availability: The rollout of 5G organizations will fundamentally influence IT framework. It will empower quicker and more solid associations, supporting a large number of uses, including expanded reality, independent vehicles, and IoT gadgets.

Serverless Figuring: Serverless registering abstracts the basic foundation completely, permitting designers to zero in exclusively on composing code. This approach works on application advancement and can prompt more savvy and versatile arrangements.

Zero Trust Security: With the rising intricacy and size of IT foundation, a Zero Trust security model is acquiring conspicuousness.

It expects that dangers can begin from the inside and outside the organization, and trust is rarely suggested. Each client and gadget is confirmed and conceded the least honor fundamental.

Manageability: As worries about natural maintainability develop, IT framework should turn out to be more energy-effective and harmless to the ecosystem. Associations will be feeling the squeeze to decrease their carbon impression and embrace green server farm advancements.

Strength and Debacle Recuperation: With the developing recurrence of cyberattacks and cataclysmic events, building tough IT foundation that can endure interruptions will be a first concern. This incorporates hearty fiasco recuperation plans and the capacity to failover to elective server farms or cloud districts.

2. **The Rise of Cloud Computing**

In the chronicles of mechanical history, scarcely any developments an affect the manner in which we live and function as distributed computing. Throughout the course of recent many years, distributed computing has developed from a promising idea into a pervasive power that pervades practically every feature of our computerized presence. It has reshaped enterprises, changed plans of action, and modified the manner in which we see and collaborate with innovation. In this investigation, we dig into the surprising ascent of distributed computing, following its beginnings, graphing its development, and looking at the extraordinary power it employs over our advanced world.

Beginnings of Distributed computing

To comprehend the ascent of distributed computing, it's crucial for handle its starting points and the issues it expected to address. In the beginning of figuring, associations depended on-premises servers and centralized computers to store and handle information. These frameworks were costly to buy and keep up with, and they frequently sat inactive for huge segments of the day, underutilized.

Distributed computing arose as an answer for these shortcomings. It planned to give figuring assets as a help, similar as power or water. As opposed to buying and overseeing actual equipment, associations could take advantage of a common pool of assets facilitated by third-get-together suppliers. This idea made ready for the introduction of distributed computing.

The Introduction of Cloud Suppliers

The last part of the 2000s saw the rise of the principal significant cloud suppliers, making way for the fast climb of distributed computing. Amazon Web Administrations (AWS), sent off in 2006, is frequently credited with promoting the cloud. AWS offered a set-up of administrations that permitted associations to lease virtual servers, stockpiling, and data sets on a pay-more only as costs arise premise. This utility-based model dispensed with the requirement for forthright capital uses and gave the versatility expected to fulfill fluctuating needs.

Following AWS, other tech goliaths like Microsoft and Google entered the cloud market with Sky blue and Google Cloud Stage, individually. These suppliers extended the extent of cloud administrations, offering many apparatuses and answers for engineers, organizations, and ventures.

Key Drivers of Cloud Reception

Cost Proficiency: Distributed computing vowed to decrease IT framework costs essentially. Associations could stay away from the forthright interest in equipment and the continuous costs of upkeep and overhauls.

Versatility: The cloud's capacity to increase assets or down on request was a unique advantage. This flexibility permitted associations to deal with top jobs without overprovisioning assets during calmer periods.

Adaptability and Spryness: Cloud administrations offered unrivaled adaptability. Designers could turn up virtual machines, send applications, and investigation with new advances rapidly and without any problem. This deftness sped up development.

Worldwide Reach: Cloud suppliers laid out server farms in different districts around the world, empowering associations to send applications and administrations nearer to their clients, decreasing idleness and further developing the client experience.

Availability: Distributed computing democratized admittance to cutting edge innovations. New companies and private ventures accessed the very incredible assets and foundation that were once the elite area of huge endeavors.

Security and Consistence: Cloud suppliers put vigorously in safety efforts and consistence confirmations, mollifying worries about information assurance and administrative consistence.

The Effect on Businesses

Data Innovation: IT divisions have moved their concentration from overseeing equipment to administering cloud administrations, stressing cloud engineering, security, and streamlining.

Business and Business: The cloud has brought the boundaries down to passage for new companies and independent ventures, empowering them to contend on a worldwide scale. The membership based model permits associations to scale as they develop.

Medical services: Distributed computing has altered medical services by working with the capacity and sharing of electronic wellbeing records, empowering telemedicine, and fueling progressed investigation for exploration and analysis.

Training: Cloud-based learning stages have become universal, permitting understudies to get to instructive assets from anyplace with a web association.

Amusement: Real time features, controlled by cloud foundation, have changed the manner in which we consume media, from music to films and gaming.

Producing: The cloud has worked with brilliant assembling, empowering continuous checking and prescient support of hardware on manufacturing plant floors.

Retail: Web based business stages and stock administration frameworks depend on cloud administrations to deal with exchanges, stock, and client information.

Arising Patterns

Multi-Cloud and Cross breed Cloud: Numerous associations are embracing multi-cloud and half and half cloud procedures to use the qualities of different cloud suppliers and organization models.

Edge Figuring: Edge registering is stretching out cloud assets to the edge of organizations, empowering constant handling for applications like IoT, independent vehicles, and increased reality.

Serverless Figuring: Serverless models conceptual server the executives completely, permitting designers to zero in on code without agonizing over foundation.

Man-made consciousness and AI: Cloud suppliers are incorporating computer based intelligence and ML administrations, making these innovations more open and strong for a more extensive scope of utilizations.

The ascent of distributed computing has been completely groundbreaking. It has moved the worldview of IT framework, offering associations the apparatuses and capacities to enhance, scale, and contend in an undeniably advanced world. Distributed computing's development indicates that things are not pulling back, and as arising advancements keep on converging with the cloud, the opportunities for future advancement are boundless. In numerous ways, the narrative of distributed computing is as yet being composed, and its impact on our reality is simply starting to be completely understood.

3. **Purpose and Scope of the Book**

In the dynamic and steadily developing domain of data innovation, understanding the reason and extent of a book is urgent to see the value in its importance and pertinence. "Cloud-First Procedures: The Fate of IT Foundation in India" isn't simply an assortment of pages bound together; it is a guide, an aide, and an investigation into a critical part of India's computerized change. In this part, we dive into the reason and extent of this book, enlightening its goals, ideal interest group, and the immense scene it envelops.

1. **Figuring out the Advanced Change Basic**
   The basic role of this book is to take apart and explain the advanced change basic in India. It fills in as a central prologue to the scene in which cloud-first procedures work. Perusers will acquire a significant comprehension of why computerized change is at this point not a choice yet a need. We investigate how the union of elements, for example, portable expansion, information examination, and government drives like Computerized India have shot India into a computerized period where IT foundation assumes an essential part.

2. **Embracing Cloud-First Methodologies**
   At the core of this book lies the idea of cloud-first methodologies. Its motivation is to demystify this idea, make sense of its importance, and grandstand how it engages associations to accomplish deftness, versatility, and advancement. Perusers will find the reason why cloud-first isn't simply a popular expression yet an essential change in IT thinking. Through certifiable models and contextual analyses, the book shows the extraordinary force of embracing cloud-first methodologies.

3. **Investigating Cloud Administration and Sending Models**
   To explore the perplexing scene of distributed computing, perusers should comprehend the different cloud administration models (IaaS, PaaS, SaaS) and sending models (public, private, mixture, multi-cloud). This book furnishes perusers with the information expected to arrive at educated conclusions about the right blend regarding administrations and arrangement models to meet India's extraordinary necessities.

4. **Tending to Information Protection and Security**
   Information protection and security are fundamental worries in India's

computerized change venture. The book's motivation is to reveal insight into these issues, exploring the intricacies of information insurance regulations and guidelines. It stresses the basic job of cloud suppliers in guaranteeing information security and consistence.

5. **Embracing Mixture and Multi-Cloud Methodologies**
   The extent of this book stretches out to cross breed and multi-cloud methodologies, perceiving the developing pattern of associations looking for a decent way to deal with cloud reception. Through contextual investigations and master bits of knowledge, perusers will get a handle on the benefits and difficulties of these methodologies and figure out how to successfully oversee intricacy.

6. **The Job of Cloud-Local Advances and Developments**
   Cloud-local innovations, including compartments, serverless, and microservices, are molding the eventual fate of IT foundation. This book investigates their part in changing India's computerized scene. Perusers will acquire experiences into how these advancements enable associations to improve and scale quickly.

7. **Crossing over the Cloud Abilities Hole**
   The book recognizes the major problem of the cloud abilities hole in India. Its motivation is to feature the significance of abilities advancement and labor force change. It gives direction on upskilling the Indian labor force to satisfy the needs of a cloud-driven world.

8. **Displaying Cloud Examples of overcoming adversity**
   Through a variety of contextual analyses, this book exhibits cloud examples of overcoming adversity in India. Perusers will gain from driving associations that have actually embraced cloud-first techniques and find the illustrations gained and key important points from their excursions.

9. **Exploring Difficulties and Traps**
   The book's extension stretches out to tending to normal difficulties in cloud reception and giving systems to relieve gambles. By analyzing best practices and keeping away from normal entanglements, associations in India can set out on their cloud-first excursion with certainty.

10. **Looking into What's to come**
    In the last sections, the book looks into the fate of distributed computing in India. It expects to arise advances, administrative changes, and the developing job of cloud-first methodologies in quite a while's computerized future.

11. **Suggestions and Significant Experiences**
    As a viable manual, "Cloud-First Methodologies" finishes up by giving suggestions and noteworthy experiences. Perusers will find how to foster a cloud-first guide, fabricate a convincing business case for cloud reception, guarantee information security and consistence, and sustain a cloud-driven culture inside their associations.

12. **Interest group**

Business Pioneers: Leaders and chiefs trying to comprehend the essential significance of cloud-first methodologies in accomplishing computerized change and acquiring an upper hand.

IT Experts: IT directors, overseers, and draftsmen hoping to explore the intricacies of cloud reception, framework improvement, and security.

New companies and Business people: Trying and existing business people expecting to use cloud-first techniques to improve, scale quickly, and contend on a worldwide scale.

Scholastics and Understudies: Teachers, scientists, and understudies in innovation related fields looking for an extensive comprehension of distributed computing and its suggestions.

Strategy Producers and Government Authorities: People engaged with molding India's advanced approaches and drives, including those connected with information assurance, security, and cloud reception.

Anyone with any interest in India's Advanced Change: Perusers keen on India's computerized venture and the job of cloud-first techniques in quite a while future.

D. Key Objectives

In the perplexing embroidery of a far reaching book like "Cloud-First Methodologies: The Eventual fate of IT Foundation in India," clear and characterized goals act as directing stars, coordinating the concentration and motivation behind each part and segment. These key goals give a guide to both the writers and the perusers, guaranteeing that the book satisfies its central goal as an enlightening and commonsense asset. In this segment, we dig into the key targets that support the book's design and content, illustrating what perusers can hope to accomplish through its pages.

1. **Far reaching Comprehension of Cloud-First Systems:**
   The essential target of the book is to give perusers a thorough comprehension of cloud-first systems. It plans to demystify this idea, making sense of its importance with regards to India's computerized change. Perusers will acquire a profound enthusiasm for why embracing cloud-first methodologies is basic for associations of all sizes and enterprises.

2. **Investigation of India's Advanced Change Basic:**
   A focal goal is to investigate and explain the computerized change basic in India. The book sets the stage by featuring the variables driving this change, from portable expansion to government drives like Advanced India. Perusers will acquire experiences into why India is at the very front of the computerized transformation and why IT framework assumes a critical part.

3. **Top to bottom Assessment of Cloud Administration and Arrangement Models:**
   Understanding the complex scene of distributed computing is a basic goal. The book digs into cloud administration models (IaaS, PaaS, SaaS) and sending

models (public, private, half and half, multi-cloud) to outfit perusers with the information expected to settle on educated conclusions about the right blend regarding administrations and arrangement models for their particular necessities.

4. **Information Protection and Security in India's Specific circumstance:** Guaranteeing information protection and security in the Indian scene is a central goal. The book tends to the intricacies of information assurance regulations and guidelines one of a kind to India, offering direction on how cloud suppliers assume a pivotal part in guaranteeing information security and consistence.

5. **Tackling the Force of Half and half and Multi-Cloud Techniques:** Perceiving the developing pattern of associations looking for a fair way to deal with cloud reception, another key goal is to investigate half and half and multi-cloud techniques. Perusers will acquire bits of knowledge into the benefits and difficulties of these procedures and figure out how to successfully oversee intricacy.

6. **Exploring the Universe of Cloud-Local Advances and Developments:** The book plans to engage perusers with the information on how cloud-local innovations, including compartments, serverless, and microservices, are reshaping IT framework. It investigates how these innovations empower associations to improve, scale quickly, and remain serious in a cloud-driven world.

7. **Tending to the Cloud Abilities Hole in India:** Abilities improvement and labor force change are basic goals. The book recognizes the major problem of the cloud abilities hole in India and gives direction on upskilling the labor force to fulfill the needs of a cloud-driven future.

8. **Exhibiting True Cloud Examples of overcoming adversity:** A fundamental goal is to motivate and illuminate through true contextual investigations. By exhibiting driving associations that have actually embraced cloud-first methodologies, perusers will acquire significant bits of knowledge into the down to earth use of these methodologies across different enterprises.

9. **Moderating Difficulties and Keeping away from Normal Entanglements:** Tending to normal difficulties in cloud reception and giving methodologies to moderate dangers is an essential goal. The book analyzes best practices and offers direction on staying away from normal traps, empowering associations to set out on their cloud-first excursion with certainty.

10. **Getting ready for the Fate of Distributed computing in India:** The book's last goal is to look into what's in store. It expects to arise advancements, administrative changes, and the developing job of cloud-first techniques in quite a while's computerized future. Perusers will acquire experiences into how to get ready for what lies ahead.

11. **Enabling a Different Crowd:**

Eventually, the book's overall goal is to engage a different crowd. From business pioneers to IT experts, business visionaries to strategy producers, and understudies to innovation lovers, the book tries to give important information and experiences that take special care of many perusers with fluctuating foundations and interests.

E. Overview of Chapters

A very much organized book resembles an efficient excursion, with every section addressing a particular waypoint on the way to figuring out, learning, and disclosure. On account of "Cloud-First Techniques: The Eventual fate of IT Framework in India," the parts are painstakingly created to direct perusers through the complicated scene of distributed computing and its job in India's computerized change. In this segment, we give an outline of the sections, featuring their critical subjects and commitments to the general account.

Part 1: The Advanced Change Basic in India

The excursion starts with an investigation of the computerized change basic in India. This primary section sets the stage by featuring the variables driving India's advanced transformation, including portable multiplication, online business development, and government drives like Computerized India. Perusers will acquire bits of knowledge into why India is at the very front of the computerized age and why IT foundation assumes an essential part.

Section 2: Embracing Cloud-First Methodologies

Section 2 digs into the core of the book's subject: cloud-first methodologies. It demystifies this idea and makes sense of its importance with regards to India's advanced change. Perusers will find the reason why cloud-first isn't simply a popular expression however an essential change in IT thinking. Certifiable models and contextual investigations represent the extraordinary force of embracing cloud-first techniques.

Part 3: Understanding Cloud Administration and Sending Models

To explore the intricacies of distributed computing, Section 3 gives a top to bottom assessment of cloud administration models (IaaS, PaaS, SaaS) and sending models (public, private, half breed, multi-cloud). This part outfits perusers with the information expected to settle on educated conclusions about the right blend regarding administrations and organization models to meet India's novel requirements.

Part 4: Information Protection and Security in India's Specific situation

Information protection and security are central worries in India's advanced change venture. Part 4 tends to these intricacies, exploring the landscape of information assurance regulations and guidelines exceptional to India. It underscores the basic job of cloud suppliers in guaranteeing information security and consistence.

Part 5: Outfitting the Force of Half and half and Multi-Cloud Procedures

Perceiving the developing pattern of associations looking for a reasonable way to deal with cloud reception, Part 5 investigates half and half and multi-cloud procedures. Perusers will acquire experiences into the benefits and difficulties of these techniques and figure out how to really oversee intricacy.

Part 6: Cloud-Local Advancements and Developments

Part 6 digs into the universe of cloud-local innovations, including compartments, serverless, and microservices. It investigates how these advances are reshaping IT foundation and empowering associations to develop, scale quickly, and remain serious in a cloud-driven world.

Part 7: Tending to the Cloud Abilities Hole in India

Abilities improvement and labor force change become the dominant focal point in Part 7. The part recognizes the major problem of the cloud abilities hole in India and gives direction on upskilling the labor force to satisfy the needs of a cloud-driven future.

Part 8: Displaying Genuine Cloud Examples of overcoming adversity

Persuasive and enlightening, Part 8 grandstands certifiable contextual investigations of associations that have actually embraced cloud-first techniques. Perusers will acquire significant experiences into the useful use of these methodologies across different enterprises.

Part 9: Moderating Difficulties and Keeping away from Normal Entanglements

Section 9 tends to normal difficulties in cloud reception and gives systems to alleviate chances. By analyzing best practices and offering direction on staying away from normal traps, the section empowers associations to set out on their cloud-first excursion with certainty.

Part 10: Looking into the Eventual fate of Distributed computing in India

The book's penultimate part looks into what's to come. Part 10 expects to arise advances, administrative changes, and the developing job of cloud-first techniques in quite a while's computerized future. Perusers will acquire experiences into how to get ready for what lies ahead.

Part 11: Suggestions and Noteworthy Experiences

As a pragmatic manual, the book closes with Section 11, giving proposals and noteworthy bits of knowledge. Perusers will find how to foster a cloud-first guide, fabricate a convincing business case for cloud reception, guarantee information security and consistence, and sustain a cloud-driven culture inside their associations.

Part 12: End - Outlining the Way ahead

The last part fills in as a finish of the book's excursion. It blends key focal points, features the significance of cloud-first methodologies in Quite a while's computerized change, and urges perusers to diagram their own way ahead in the cloud-driven scene.

Chapter 1

The Digital Transformation Imperative

The Advanced Change Basic

In the records of mankind's set of experiences, barely any powers have reshaped the world as essentially as the advanced upset. The 21st century is set apart by a period of extraordinary innovative progression, where the computerized change basic isn't simply a decision however a need for people, associations, and countries.

The rise of the web in the late twentieth century denoted a vital crossroads in mankind's set of experiences. It was the origin of a world-wide organization that would interface billions of individuals, gadgets, and frameworks, changing the manner in which we convey, work, and live. The web's unassuming starting points as an exploration project have developed into a rambling computerized biological system that supports essentially every part of current life.

As the web's scope extended, it carried with it an influx of developments that reclassified businesses and tested ordinary standards. The appearance of cell phones reformed individualized computing, placing the force of the web in the pockets of billions. Distributed computing democratized admittance to figuring assets, permitting organizations to scale and enhance without the weight of broad framework.

The Web of Things (IoT) associated regular items to the web, empowering shrewd homes, urban communities, and businesses. Man-made brainpower (computer based intelligence) and AI (ML) turned into the main impetus behind information examination, robotization, and customized encounters. Blockchain innovation guaranteed new degrees of safety and straightforwardness in monetary exchanges and supply chains.

In this computerized age, information arose as the new cash, and network safety turned into a foremost concern. The ascent of web-based entertainment changed correspondence and data scattering, reshaping the media scene and affecting worldwide occasions. Web based business disturbed conventional retail, and the gig economy changed the idea of work.

India's Rising in the Computerized World

While the computerized change wave cleared across the globe, India arose as a huge player in this advanced renaissance. The country's excursion into the computerized age is portrayed by dramatic development, quick reception of innovation, and a dream to use computerized instruments for cultural and monetary turn of events.

India's computerized venture started with the advancement of its economy during the 1990s, which laid the basis for the data innovation (IT) and programming administrations industry to thrive. The country's IT ability before long became apparent on the worldwide stage, with Indian IT organizations giving re-appropriating administrations to organizations around the world.

The expansion of cell phones in the mid 21st century democratized admittance to data and correspondence. India's assorted populace embraced portable innovation, jumping conventional figuring to enter the versatile time straightforwardly. Today, India brags one the biggest cell phone client bases on the planet.

The public authority of India perceived the extraordinary capability of advanced innovations and sent off visionary drives to speed up the country's computerized change. The "Advanced India" crusade, sent off in 2015, expected to connect the computerized partition, enable residents carefully, and change administration through innovation. It visualized a carefully comprehensive India where each resident approached fundamental administrations and data on the web.

All the while, the "Make in India" drive looked to advance assembling and development inside the country. It planned to situate India as a worldwide assembling center, cultivating business venture and occupation creation in areas like gadgets and equipment.

The Advanced Change Basic in India

The computerized change basic in India isn't just determined by a longing to embrace the most recent mechanical patterns; supported by convincing reasons and objectives contact each feature of society and the economy.

Financial Development and Incorporation

At its center, advanced change is about monetary development and consideration. It's tied in with tackling the force of innovation to drive monetary advancement, make occupations, and elevate underserved networks. In India, this basic is especially articulated.

The computerized economy in India is flourishing, contributing altogether to the country's Gross domestic product. It incorporates a wide range of businesses, from web based business and IT administrations to fintech and computerized diversion. New companies are expanding, drawing in venture from both homegrown and worldwide sources. The advanced economy isn't restricted to metropolitan focuses; it's entering rustic regions, setting out open doors and diminishing local incongruities.

One of the vital drivers of monetary development in the computerized period is business. India's startup biological system has earned worldwide respect for its dynamic quality and advancement. Business visionaries are utilizing advanced innovations to upset customary enterprises and address cultural difficulties. The soul of business venture isn't restricted to a limited handful; it's spreading the country over, with new companies rising up out of more modest towns and urban communities.

Computerized change is likewise an impetus for work creation. The IT and IT-empowered administrations industry stays a critical boss, however new open doors are emerging in arising advances like man-made intelligence, information examination, and online protection. The gig economy, controlled by computerized stages, is changing the idea of work, turning out adaptable revenue open doors to millions.

Significantly, advanced incorporation is fundamental to India's development story. The public authority's endeavors to advance computerized education and network are crucial in guaranteeing that the advantages of the advanced economy arrive at all sections of society. Monetary consideration, through drives like Jan Dhan Yojana and the Brought together Installments Connection point (UPI), is enabling the unbanked and oppressed to take part in the proper economy.

Government Drives

The Indian government has been instrumental in driving the advanced change basic. It perceives that computerized advancements are apparatuses for proficiency as well as empowering agents of comprehensive development and great administration.

The "Computerized India" crusade, sent off by Top state leader Narendra Modi in 2015, is a lead drive that exemplifies India's obligation to computerized change. The program's vision is to change India into a carefully engaged society and information economy. It centers around key regions like framework advancement, computerized proficiency, e-administration, and online protection.

Under the Advanced India program, a few extraordinary ventures have been sent off. The BharatNet project plans to give broadband availability to each town in India. The Public Computerized Wellbeing Mission looks to make a computerized wellbeing environment, guaranteeing open and proficient medical care administrations for all residents.

E-administration drives have worked on taxpayer supported organizations, lessening organization and defilement. The Computerized Storage framework permits residents to electronically store and offer significant records. The Bound together Installments Connection point (UPI) has reformed advanced installments, making exchanges consistent and comprehensive.

Notwithstanding Computerized India, the "Make in India" drive supports homegrown assembling and development. It looks to establish a climate helpful for venture and occupation creation in areas like gadgets, media communications, and environmentally friendly power. By advancing neighborhood assembling and diminishing import reliance, Make in India plans to support confidence and financial versatility.

These administration drives are not secluded endeavors but rather an intelligible procedure to use computerized innovations for public turn of events.

They exhibit a pledge to outfitting development, cultivating business, and guaranteeing that the advantages of computerized change arrive at each resident.

Business venture and New companies

India's computerized change story is fragmented without praising the business visionaries and new companies that are driving advancement and interruption. These pioneers are adding to monetary development as well as impacting the manner in which India and the world see mechanical potential outcomes.

The Indian startup environment has seen hazardous development in the previous 10 years. It's not generally restricted to a couple of metropolitan center points; new companies are rising up out of level 2 and level 3 urban communities, taking advantage of neighborhood ability and tending to local difficulties.

Online business monsters like Flipkart and Amazon India have reshaped retail, making it more helpful and open to shoppers. Food conveyance stages like Zomato and Swiggy have changed eating propensities. Edtech new companies are altering instruction, offering customized learning answers for understudies the nation over.

Fintech developments are democratizing finance. Portable installment stages like Paytm and PhonePe have made computerized exchanges a lifestyle. Shared loaning stages are giving admittance to credit to people and independent ventures.

Healthtech new companies are further developing medical services access and conveyance. Telemedicine stages associate patients with specialists from a distance, decreasing the weight on medical care framework. Clinical diagnostics and wellbeing GPS beacons are engaging people to assume responsibility for their prosperity.

Advancements in agritech are assisting ranchers with upgrading efficiency and diminish post-collect misfortunes. Brilliant water system frameworks, crop checking utilizing satellites, and computerized commercial centers are changing farming.

Man-made brainpower and information examination new companies are driving experiences and proficiency across ventures. They are assisting organizations with settling on information driven choices, mechanize cycles, and upgrade client encounters.

The soul of business is flourishing in India, upheld by a strong environment of funding, private supporters, and hatcheries. Government drives like Startup India give a favorable climate to new businesses to prosper, offering motivating forces, financing open doors, and mentorship.

India's new businesses are not simply centered around the homegrown market; they are growing universally, exhibiting Indian advancement and innovation on the world stage. Their examples of overcoming adversity motivate another age of business visionaries, supporting the computerized change basic.

Advanced Consideration and Access

The advanced change basic in India reaches out past monetary development and business venture; it is generally about consideration and access. It perceives that the advantages of the computerized time ought to arrive at each edge of the country, connecting partitions and decreasing abberations.

Foundation Bottlenecks

While India's computerized venture is set apart by victories, it isn't absent any trace of difficulties. Framework bottlenecks have been a longstanding issue. Lacking broadband network in country and distant regions has obstructed web access for millions. Regardless of progress, there is as yet a requirement for additional server farms to help the developing computerized biological system.

Online protection Concerns

The advanced age has introduced new weaknesses. Online protection dangers have become more modern and inescapable. Guaranteeing the security of computerized foundation and information is a fundamental concern. India's establishments, both public and private, should ceaselessly adjust and put resources into strong online protection measures.

Information Protection and Guideline

Information protection and guideline are perplexing issues in the advanced period. India has done whatever it may take to address these worries through the Individual Information Assurance Bill, which expects to defend people's information while advancing advancement and financial development. Offsetting protection with the requirement for information driven administrations is a continuous test.

Advanced Education

Computerized education is a foundation of advanced consideration. While progress has been made, there is as yet a need to improve computerized education among residents, particularly in rustic and underserved regions. Schooling and preparing programs are fundamental to enable people to successfully explore the advanced world.

The computerized change basic in India is a multi-layered venture set apart by development, advancement, and inclusivity. It addresses the country's obligation to utilizing innovation for monetary turn of events, great administration, and cultural advancement.

India's climb in the computerized world is a demonstration of its versatility, flexibility, and pioneering soul. It is an account of billions of people outfitting the force of network, development, and computerized instruments to shape their fates.

While challenges exist, they are potential open doors for development and improvement. Foundation advancement, network safety measures, information security, and computerized education are regions where purposeful endeavors will yield significant advantages.

As India proceeds with its advanced change venture, it fills in as a motivation to countries around the world. It shows that computerized change is definitely not a decision yet a goal — one that can prompt a more splendid, more comprehensive future for all. The advanced age has shown up, and India is prepared to embrace its maximum capacity.

1.1 The Acceleration of Digital Transformation

The 21st century has been set apart by a quick and constant rush of innovative headway that has pervaded each feature of our lives. This constant walk of advancement has on a very basic level modified the manner in which we live, work, and interface with our general surroundings. At the core of this change lies the peculiarity known as computerized change, a broad cycle that has picked up exceptional speed lately. In this investigation spreading over 1000 words, we set out on an excursion through the speeding up powers behind computerized change, its significant effect on organizations and society, and the techniques to explore this fast track to what's in store.

1. The Impetuses of Speed increase

1.1. The Worldwide Pandemic: A Distinct advantage

The first and maybe most huge impetus for the speed increase of advanced change has been the worldwide Coronavirus pandemic. The pandemic constrained associations across the globe to quickly adjust to remote work, web based learning, and advanced correspondence. Organizations that had recently been reluctant to embrace computerized advances were unexpectedly constrained to do as such to make due and flourish in a universe of lockdowns and social separating.

Remote work and cooperation devices, distributed computing, and online business experienced unstable development as organizations looked for ways of proceeding with tasks in a virtual climate. The pandemic showed the versatility of advanced innovations and highlighted their fundamental job in keeping up with business congruity.

1.2. Progressions in Innovation: The Advanced Tool kit

Headways in innovation have been one more significant driver of advanced change speed increase. Advancements like man-made brainpower (simulated intelligence), AI, and mechanization have arrived at new levels of complexity and openness. These innovations are all the more impressive as well as more reasonable, making them open to associations, everything being equal.

Distributed computing has turned into the foundation of advanced framework, offering versatility, adaptability, and cost-adequacy. The Web of Things (IoT) has extended its scope, interfacing billions of gadgets and empowering information driven navigation. 5G organizations are ready to reform availability, opening ways to low-inertness, high-transfer speed applications.

Blockchain innovation is building up forward momentum, promising improved security and straightforwardness in different businesses, from money to store network the board. Quantum processing, however still in its outset, holds the possibility to tackle complex issues at speeds impossible with old style PCs.

1.3. Information as the New Money

Information has arisen as the new money of the advanced age. The expansion of computerized gadgets and sensors has prompted a blast of information age. This information, when tackled and dissected successfully, holds the way to bits of knowledge, advancement, and upper hand.

The ascent of huge information examination, combined with

artificial intelligence and AI, has empowered associations to extricate important bits of knowledge from tremendous datasets. These bits of knowledge drive navigation, improve client encounters, and advance activities. Information driven associations are better prepared to adjust to changing economic situations and remain in front of the opposition.

2. Influence on Business and Society

2.1. Changing Plans of action

The speed increase of computerized change has significantly affected plans of action across businesses. Customary physical organizations have needed to turn to web based business and online conveyance models. The membership economy, portrayed by administrations like Netflix and Spotify, has acquired unmistakable quality.

Computerized stages have upset enterprises, taking into consideration the immediate association of makers and purchasers. The gig economy has prospered, turning out adaptable revenue open doors for millions. Organizations have moved from item driven to client driven models, utilizing information to comprehend and take care of individual inclinations.

2.2. Reshaping Client Encounters

Client encounters have been changed by advanced innovations. Online business has changed shopping, proposing customized suggestions and consistent exchanges. Computer generated reality (VR) and increased reality (AR) are improving vivid encounters, from gaming to land.

Chatbots and remote helpers are giving moment client care, further developing reaction times and effectiveness. Online entertainment stages have become fundamental for brand commitment and advertising. Versatile applications and sites have become essential touchpoints for organizations to interface with clients.

2.3. Empowering Remote Work and Coordinated effort

The pandemic constrained a change in perspective in the manner we work. Remote work and cooperation devices have turned into the standard, empowering groups to cooperate from anyplace on the planet. Video conferencing stages like Zoom and Microsoft Groups have seen touchy development.

Cloud-based efficiency instruments like Google Work area and Microsoft 365 have engaged telecommuters to team up consistently on archives and undertakings. Associations have needed to put resources into secure remote access arrangements and network safety measures to safeguard their advanced resources.

2.4. Improving Medical services and Instruction

The speed increase of computerized change essentially affects medical services and instruction. Telemedicine has flooded, permitting patients to remotely talk with medical care suppliers. Remote checking gadgets and wellbeing applications are empowering people to proactively deal with their wellbeing more.

In training, e-learning stages have become fundamental for remote and mixture learning models. Instructive innovation (EdTech) arrangements are giving customized opportunities for growth and extending admittance to schooling all around the world. Virtual homerooms and computerized reading material are reshaping the manner in which understudies learn.

3. Exploring the Fast track to What's to come

3.1. Embrace a Computerized First Outlook

In the period of computerized change speed increase, associations should take on an advanced first mentality. This implies focusing on advanced innovations and systems in all parts of business tasks. Pioneers should support advanced drives and guarantee that they are incorporated into the association's DNA.

3.2. Put resources into Advanced Abilities and Preparing

To explore the fast track of computerized change, associations should put resources into the improvement of advanced abilities and preparing for their labor force. Representatives should be furnished with the information and capacities to really use computerized devices. Constant learning and upskilling ought to be supported.

3.3. Secure Advanced Framework

As advanced change speeds up, the significance of online protection couldn't possibly be more significant. Associations should focus on the security of their computerized foundation and information. Vigorous network safety measures, including encryption, multifaceted confirmation, and standard security reviews, are fundamental to safeguard against digital dangers.

3.4. Influence Information Investigation and artificial intelligence

Information investigation and artificial intelligence can possibly drive advancement and upper hand. Associations ought to use these innovations to separate noteworthy experiences from their information. Artificial intelligence can mechanize processes, improve direction, and make customized client encounters.

3.5. Adjust to Changing Client Assumptions

Client assumptions are advancing quickly in the computerized age. Associations should remain receptive to these progressions and adjust their procedures as needs be. Paying attention to client criticism, observing patterns, and embracing a client driven approach are significant for progress.

The speed increase of computerized change is a dynamic and constant power reshaping organizations and society at an uncommon speed. It is driven by a juncture of variables, including the worldwide pandemic, progressions in innovation, and the acknowledgment of information's worth.

This speed increase has changed plans of action, reshaped client encounters, and empowered remote work and coordinated effort. It has additionally improved medical services and training, giving new open doors and difficulties.

To explore this fast track to the future, associations should embrace a computerized first mentality, put resources into computerized abilities, secure their computerized foundation, influence information examination and man-made intelligence, and adjust to changing client assumptions.

The computerized change basic isn't simply a pattern; a major shift will keep on forming our reality before long. The people who embrace it with nimbleness and foreknowledge will be best situated to flourish in the carefully changed scene.

1.2 The Indian Context

As the world plunges forward in the period of advanced change, it is fundamental to perceive that the material whereupon this epochal shift unfurls isn't uniform. The speed, elements, and difficulties of advanced change differ essentially across countries and locales. Inside this different scene, India arises as an especially convincing and complex setting, where a conjunction of variables has led to a computerized change story that is however rich as it could be interesting. In this investigation spreading over 1000 words, we dive into the Indian setting of computerized change, disentangling the country's particular attributes, potential open doors, and difficulties on its excursion into the advanced age.

1. Socioeconomics and Computerized Reception
1.1. A Young Populace

India's segment profile is a basic calculate forming its computerized change venture. With a populace of over 1.3 billion, India is home to one of the world's biggest youth populaces. The greater part of its residents are younger than 25, making it an energetic country with massive potential for computerized reception and development.

This segment profit has filled the quick reception of computerized advances, especially among the more youthful age. India's childhood are early adopters of cell phones, virtual entertainment, and advanced administrations, driving patterns in web based business, person to person communication, and online substance utilization.

1.2. Crossing over the Advanced Gap

While the metropolitan youth have embraced computerized innovations eagerly, there stays an advanced split among metropolitan and provincial India. Metropolitan regions have better admittance to rapid web, cell phones, and advanced foundation, while country areas actually face network difficulties.

The Indian government has perceived the significance of spanning this gap through drives like BharatNet, which expects to give broadband network to country regions. Connecting the computerized partition isn't just a question of openness yet additionally of guaranteeing that the advantages of advanced change arrive at all fragments of society.

2. Government Drives: Computerized India and Then some

2.1. Computerized India: A Visionary Drive

The public authority of India plays had a urgent impact in catalyzing computerized change through its visionary drive, "Computerized India." Sent off in 2015, Advanced India looks to change the country into a carefully enabled society and information economy. The program's multi-layered approach incorporates key regions like computerized foundation, e-administration, advanced proficiency, and network safety.

Under Computerized India, a few extraordinary tasks have been sent off, including BharatNet, which intends to give broadband network to each town, and the Public Computerized Wellbeing Mission, which looks to make a computerized wellbeing environment. These drives have further developed admittance to advanced administrations as well as improved straightforwardness and proficiency in government tasks.

2.2. Advancing Advancement: Make in India

Advancement and business venture are fundamental to India's computerized change story. The "Make in India" drive, sent off in 2014, energizes homegrown assembling, advancement, and venture. It tries to situate India as a worldwide assembling center, encouraging business and occupation creation in areas like hardware, broadcast communications, and sustainable power.

The Startup India program supplements this drive by advancing a culture of development and business venture. It offers motivating forces, subsidizing open doors, and mentorship to new companies, sustaining a flourishing biological system of computerized pioneers.

3. **Computerized Economy: Internet business and Fintech**

3.1. Web based business Upset

India's web based business scene has seen a significant change lately. Internet business stages like Flipkart, Amazon India, and Snapdeal have disturbed customary retail, offering buyers a great many items and administrations with the comfort of doorstep conveyance.

The development of web based business has been additionally advanced by the multiplication of cell phones and reasonable versatile information plans. Portable business (m-trade) has become progressively predominant, with purchasers utilizing their cell phones to shop, cover bills, and access a heap of computerized administrations.

3.2. Fintech Advancement

The fintech area in India has seen surprising development and development. Computerized installment stages like Paytm, PhonePe, and research Pay have upset how exchanges are led. The Bound together Installments Point of interaction (UPI) has turned into a universal and proficient installment framework, working with shared and trader exchanges.

Past installments, fintech new businesses are venturing into regions like computerized loaning, protection, and abundance the board. These developments are upgrading monetary consideration as well as trying customary banking and monetary administrations suppliers to adjust and enhance.

4. New companies and Advancement Center points

4.1. Flourishing Startup Biological system

India's startup biological system has earned worldwide respect for its liveliness and development. The nation is home to a developing number of new companies across different areas, from web based business and fintech to healthtech and edtech.

Urban communities like Bengaluru, frequently alluded to as the "Silicon Valley of India," have arisen as advancement center points, drawing in ability, financial backers, and business people. The startup biological system is described by hatcheries, gas pedals, investment firms, and a culture of hazard taking.

Indian new companies are serving the homegrown market as well as growing universally, displaying Indian advancement on the world stage. Their examples of overcoming adversity move another age of business people and support India's situation as a computerized development center.

5. Difficulties and Potential open doors

5.1. Availability Challenges*

While India has gained critical headway in growing computerized foundation, availability challenges persevere, especially in rustic and distant regions. The computerized partition stays an obstruction to comprehensive advanced change. Tending to availability holes and guaranteeing reasonable web access for all residents are progressing difficulties.

5.2. Information Protection and Security*

The rising digitization of administrations and exchanges has raised worries about information security and online protection. India is currently forming information security regulations to defend people's information while advancing development and monetary development. Fortifying network safety measures is fundamental to safeguard against digital dangers.

5.3. Computerized Literacy*

Computerized proficiency is significant to guaranteeing that all portions of society can partake in the advanced economy. Endeavors to upgrade computerized proficiency, particularly in provincial and under-served regions, are fundamental for crossing over the advanced gap and engaging people to successfully explore the computerized world.

The Indian setting of computerized change is described by a young populace, government drives like Computerized India and Make in India, a flourishing advanced economy including online business and fintech, a powerful startup biological system, and special difficulties connected with network, information protection, and advanced proficiency.

India's computerized change venture is an account of monstrous potential, development, and inclusivity. While challenges exist, they are open doors for development and improvement. The country's computerized account is consistently developing, and its extraordinary setting adds dynamic quality to the worldwide embroidered artwork of advanced change. As India bridles the force of computerized innovations, it stands ready to make a permanent imprint on the advanced scene of the 21st hundred years.

1.3 Role of IT Infrastructure in Digital Transformation

In the computerized age, associations overall are going through significant changes to remain serious, important, and nimble. Key to this advancement is the outfitting of computerized advancements, information driven bits of knowledge, and mechanization to streamline processes, improve client encounters, and drive development. At the core of these computerized drives lies the IT foundation — an intricate environment of equipment, programming, organizations, and cloud administrations. This investigation, traversing 1000 words, dives into the significant job of IT framework in advanced change, analyzing how it fills in as the bedrock for the computerized upset.

1. Characterizing Advanced Change
1.1. The Advanced Insurgency

Computerized change is certainly not a solitary occasion yet a persistent interaction driven by the fast headway of advanced innovations. It envelops a principal shift in how associations work, draw in with clients, and make esteem. Computerized change outfits the force of information, availability, and computerization to accomplish key targets and keep up with seriousness.

1.2. Key Mainstays of Computerized Change

Information Investigation: Utilizing information to acquire experiences, pursue informed choices, and drive personalization.

Distributed computing: Empowering adaptable and adaptable foundation for information capacity and processing power.

Man-made consciousness (computer based intelligence) and AI (ML): Robotizing assignments, foreseeing patterns, and upgrading independent direction.

IoT (Web of Things): Interfacing gadgets and frameworks for continuous information assortment and control.

Mechanization: Smoothing out processes, diminishing manual intercession, and further developing effectiveness.

Client Centricity: Zeroing in on customized encounters and meeting client assumptions.

2. The Basic Job of IT Foundation

2.1. The Foundation of Advanced Change

IT framework shapes the underpinning of an association's computerized change venture. It incorporates both on-premises and cloud-based assets, including servers, stockpiling, systems administration, data sets, and programming. A hearty IT framework is fundamental for the effective execution of computerized drives.

2.2. Empowering Versatility and Adaptability

One of the center advantages of present day IT framework is adaptability. Distributed computing, specifically, permits associations to increase assets or down in view of interest. This adaptability is urgent for dealing with changes in information handling, client traffic, and responsibilities, guaranteeing ideal execution and cost-productivity.

2.3. Information The executives and Capacity

Computerized change relies on the successful administration and examination of information. IT framework gives the capacity and handling abilities important to gather, store, and break down huge measures of information. With the ascent of enormous information and investigation, associations depend on IT foundation to help their information driven dynamic cycles.

2.4. Cloud Administrations and Virtualization

Cloud administrations, presented by suppliers like Amazon Web Administrations (AWS), Microsoft Purplish blue, and Google Cloud, assume a significant part in computerized change. These stages give adaptable assets, decreasing the requirement for broad on-premises framework. Virtualization innovations empower associations to run various virtual machines on a solitary actual server, enhancing asset use.

2.5. Network Availability and Security

A dependable organization foundation is basic for guaranteeing network between gadgets, applications, and clients. With the expansion of remote work and IoT gadgets, network foundation should be vigorous and secure. Network security arrangements are fundamental to safeguard against digital dangers and breaks, shielding delicate information.

3. Improving Business Readiness

3.1. Speeding up Opportunity to-Market

In a computerized economy, speed is an upper hand. IT foundation that upholds quick turn of events, testing, and organization of computerized arrangements speeds up opportunity to-showcase for new items and administrations. Cloud-based conditions offer DevOps abilities, considering persistent joining and conveyance (CI/Cd) of programming.

3.2. Adjusting to Market Changes

Computerized change empowers associations to adjust rapidly to advertise changes and client inclinations. Nimble IT foundation takes into consideration the consistent coordination of new innovations and administrations. For example, associations can carry out computer based intelligence fueled chatbots for client service or IoT sensors for continuous information observing without significant disturbances.

4. **Improving Client Encounters**

4.1. Personalization and Information Examination

IT framework upholds the assortment and investigation of client information, working with customized encounters. Client relationship the board (CRM) frameworks, controlled by information examination and simulated intelligence, empower associations to tailor promoting efforts, proposals, and correspondence to individual inclinations.

4.2. Omnichannel Commitment

A powerful IT foundation empowers omnichannel commitment with clients. Whether through sites, versatile applications, virtual entertainment, or chatbots, associations can give steady and consistent encounters across various touchpoints. This further develops consumer loyalty and unwaveringness.

5. **Driving Advancement**

5.1. Trial and error and Advancement Labs

IT framework can uphold advancement labs or sandboxes, where associations try different things with arising innovations and foster confirmation of-idea projects. These labs cultivate a culture of development and give a space to testing groundbreaking thoughts without disturbing center tasks.

5.2. Simulated intelligence and AI Combination

Simulated intelligence and AI models require huge computational assets for preparing and surmising. Current IT framework, particularly cloud stages, gives the computational power and capacity limit required for man-made intelligence driven advancement. This can go from prescient investigation to regular language handling applications.

6. Difficulties and Contemplations

6.1. Cost Administration

While distributed computing offers adaptability and adaptability, it can likewise prompt startling expenses on the off chance that assets are not overseen productively. Associations should cautiously design their IT spending and screen cloud asset utilization to improve costs.

6.2. Security and Consistence

With the rising advanced impression, network protection becomes central. Associations should carry out powerful safety efforts to safeguard information and frameworks. Consistence with information insurance guidelines, like GDPR and HIPAA, is fundamental to stay away from legitimate and reputational gambles.

6.3. Inheritance Frameworks Mix

Numerous associations have inheritance IT frameworks that need to coincide with current foundation. Coordinating inheritance frameworks with more up to date advanced innovations can be mind boggling and may require particular skill.

In the time of advanced change, IT foundation is the uncelebrated yet truly great individual that supports development, readiness, and client centricity. It empowers associations to gather, make due, and break down information, adjust to changing economic situations, improve client encounters, and drive advancement.

The job of IT foundation goes past supporting advanced drives; it shapes the way of life and capacities of an association. Associations that put resources into vigorous, adaptable, and secure Flourishing in the advanced age, embracing change as a chance for development and innovation foundation are better situated. As innovation keeps on advancing, the job of IT framework in computerized change will stay focal, guaranteeing that associations can explore the steadily changing scene of the advanced transformation.

1.4 Challenges and Opportunities

In the powerful scene of computerized change, associations face a horde of difficulties and open doors. The persistent speed of innovative headway, moving client assumptions, and developing plans of action establish a climate of both interruption and potential. In this investigation spreading over 1000 words, we analyze the vital difficulties and open doors that associations experience in their excursion towards advanced change.

Challenges

1. **Inheritance Frameworks and Specialized Obligation**

   1.1. The Inheritance Problem

   Perhaps of the most unavoidable test in advanced change is managing heritage frameworks and specialized obligation. Numerous associations have collected a complicated trap of obsolete innovation, making it hard to flawlessly execute new computerized arrangements. Heritage frameworks might miss the mark on adaptability, versatility, and similarity expected to help present day advanced drives.

   1.2. Joining Intricacy

   Coordinating inheritance frameworks with new computerized stages can be an imposing errand. Similarity issues, information storehouses, and the requirement for custom connectors can obstruct the smooth progression of data and cycles. This intricacy frequently demands significant investment and assets to survive.

2. **Network protection and Information Security**

   2.1. Network protection Dangers

   The computerized period has introduced another flood of online protection dangers. Associations are continually under the danger of information breaks, ransomware assaults, and different cybercrimes. The advancing idea of these dangers expects associations to put altogether in hearty network safety measures.

   2.2. Information Security Guidelines

Information security guidelines, like GDPR in Europe and CCPA in California, have presented tough prerequisites for the assurance of individual information.

Associations should explore a complicated scene of consistence, guaranteeing that information is gathered, handled, and put away in a way that regards individual protection privileges.

3. Ability and Expertise Deficiencies

3.1. The Advanced Abilities Hole

The interest for advanced abilities far surpasses the stock of qualified ability. Associations battle to find people with aptitude in regions like information examination, man-made intelligence, network safety, and distributed computing. This ability deficiency can obstruct advanced change drives.

3.2. Nonstop Learning*

Computerized advances develop quickly. Associations should cultivate a culture of nonstop figuring out how to stay up with the latest. This requires interest in preparing and advancement programs.

4. Change The board and Culture

4.1. Protection from Change

Computerized change frequently requires a huge change in how work is finished. Representatives might oppose these changes, dreading position relocation or a lofty expectation to learn and adapt. Viable change the executives procedures are vital for address opposition and guarantee a smooth progress.

4.2. Hierarchical Culture*

Computerized change isn't just about innovation; it's about culture. Associations should develop a culture of advancement, flexibility, and client centricity. Changing profoundly imbued social standards and practices can challenge.

5. Information Over-burden

5.1. The Information Downpour

The blast of information can be both a gift and a revile. While information gives important bits of knowledge, associations can undoubtedly become overpowered by the sheer volume of data. Separating significant experiences from huge datasets requires refined information examination capacities.

Potential open doors

1. **Development and Deftness**
   1.1. Quick Advancement
   Advanced change makes the way for fast development. Associations can try different things with arising advances like man-made intelligence, IoT, and blockchain to make new items, administrations, and plans of action. These developments can give an upper hand.
   1.2. Light-footed Activities
   Computerized apparatuses and cloud-based foundation empower associations to work with dexterity. Nimble procedures, like DevOps, work with quicker advancement and sending of programming. This deftness permits associations to answer rapidly to advertise changes and client input.
2. **Upgraded Client Encounters**
   2.1. Personalization
   Computerized change empowers associations to offer exceptionally customized client encounters. By utilizing information and simulated intelligence, organizations can fit items and administrations to individual inclinations, expanding consumer loyalty and devotion.
   2.2. Omnichannel Engagement
   Omnichannel commitment permits associations to collaborate with clients flawlessly across different touchpoints, from sites and versatile applications to web-based entertainment and chatbots. This extensive methodology further develops the general client experience.

3. Information Driven Navigation

3.1. Informed Navigation

Admittance to information investigation instruments engages associations to go with information driven choices. By dissecting client conduct, market patterns, and functional information, associations can enhance processes, recognize open doors, and alleviate gambles.

3.2. Prescient Examination

Prescient examination models can gauge future patterns and results. These models aid stock administration, request estimating, and client agitate forecast, assisting associations with remaining on the ball.

4. Cost Advancement

4.1. Effectiveness Gains

Computerized change can prompt huge expense investment funds through process computerization, further developed asset distribution, and diminished difficult work.

Distributed computing permits associations to pay for assets on a utilization premise, improving IT spending.

5. Worldwide Reach

5.1. Growing Business sectors

Computerized stages and web based business empower associations to arrive at worldwide business sectors without the requirement for an actual presence in each area. This extension opens up new learning experiences and income streams.

5.2. Distant Work

Computerized change upholds remote work game plans. Associations can take advantage of a worldwide ability pool, access particular abilities, and deal adaptable work choices to representatives.

6. Maintainability

6.1. Green Advancements

Computerized change can add to supportability objectives. Distributed computing lessens the requirement for on-premises server farms, diminishing energy utilization and fossil fuel byproducts. IoT gadgets can screen and upgrade asset utilization.

Computerized change gives associations a double scene of difficulties and open doors. Inheritance frameworks, network safety dangers, ability deficiencies, and social movements are among the obstacles that should be survived. Notwithstanding, the potential for fast development, upgraded client encounters, information driven independent direction, and cost improvement offers a convincing vision representing things to come.

To outfit the chances of computerized change, associations should take on a comprehensive methodology that includes innovation, culture, and ability. They should put resources into upskilling their labor force, bracing online protection safeguards, and encouraging a culture of development and flexibility. By tending to these difficulties and immediately jumping all over chances, associations can explore the perplexing territory of advanced change and flourish in the computerized age.

Chapter 2

Understanding Cloud-First Strategies

In the present quick moving computerized scene, organizations are continually looking for ways of remaining serious and lithe. The reception of distributed computing has arisen as a crucial methodology for accomplishing these objectives. Cloud-first systems have acquired conspicuousness as associations perceive the various advantages presented by cloud advancements. This thorough investigation digs into the idea of cloud-first techniques, their importance, execution challenges, and the developing scene of distributed computing.

Presentation

The advanced upset has introduced a period where information and innovation are at the center of business activities. As organizations depend progressively on innovation to smooth out activities, interface with clients, and drive advancement, the significance of a proficient IT framework couldn't possibly be more significant. Distributed computing has arisen as an extraordinary power, offering versatile, adaptable, and practical answers for meet the developing necessities of present day endeavors.

A cloud-first system is a methodology where an association focuses on cloud answers for its innovation needs. It includes a conscious shift from conventional on-premises framework and applications to cloud-based other options. This shift is driven by the acknowledgment that distributed computing can give improved readiness, adaptability, and cost-proficiency contrasted with customary IT arrangements.

Meaning of Cloud-First Methodologies

1. **Deftness and Adaptability**

   One of the essential explanations for the reception of cloud-first techniques is the capacity to quickly increase assets or down on a case by case basis. Conventional on-premises foundation frequently requires significant lead times and capital use for scaling, making it inappropriate for organizations that need to answer rapidly to showcase changes. Cloud administrations, then again, permit associations to arrangement and de-arrangement assets on-request, empowering them to adjust to changing economic situations flawlessly.

2. **Cost Proficiency**

   Cost investment funds have been a driving element for the far reaching reception of cloud-first techniques. By disposing of the requirement for significant forthright interests in equipment and diminishing continuous support costs, distributed computing offers massive expense benefits. Also, cloud suppliers ordinarily offer pay-more only as costs arise estimating models, empowering associations to pay just for the assets they use.

3. **Advancement and Upper hand**

   Cloud-first systems enable organizations to zero in on development as opposed to framework the board. With the cloud taking care of the fundamental foundation and administrations, associations can redirect their assets and ability toward creating inventive items and administrations. This change in center can give an upper hand by speeding up opportunity to-showcase for new contributions.

4. **Availability and Joint effort**

   The cloud empowers more noteworthy availability to information and applications. This openness is especially useful for organizations with conveyed groups or far off labor forces. Cloud-based coordinated effort apparatuses and stages make it simpler for representatives to cooperate no matter what their actual area, cultivating efficiency and productivity.

5. **Calamity Recuperation and Business Progression**

Cloud administrations offer hearty calamity recuperation and business progression arrangements. By putting away information and applications in topographically excess server farms, associations can guarantee that their basic frameworks stay functional even notwithstanding catastrophic events or equipment disappointments. This upgraded versatility is a convincing motivation to take on cloud-first systems.

Carrying out a Cloud-First Technique

1. **Characterize Clear Targets**

   Start by characterizing clear targets for embracing a cloud-first procedure. These targets ought to line up with the association's general business objectives. Normal goals might incorporate decreasing IT costs, further developing readiness, upgrading information security, or speeding up advancement.

2. **Evaluate Current IT Climate**

   Prior to relocating to the cloud, lead an exhaustive evaluation of your ongoing IT climate. Distinguish existing applications, foundation, and information. This evaluation will assist you with figuring out which responsibilities are appropriate for relocation and which might require adjustments or overhaul.

3. **Pick the Right Cloud Administration Models**

   Distributed computing offers different help models, including

Framework as an Assistance (IaaS), Stage as an Assistance (PaaS), and Programming as a Help (SaaS). Assess which administration models adjust best to your association's requirements. For example, SaaS might be reasonable for offloading non-center applications, while IaaS or PaaS might be more fitting for custom improvement projects.

4. **Select the Right Cloud Suppliers**

   Pick cloud suppliers that line up with your association's prerequisites and targets. Consider factors, for example, the supplier's worldwide presence, server farm areas, consistence accreditations, and evaluating models. Numerous associations decide on multi-cloud or mixture cloud methodologies to use the qualities of various cloud suppliers.

5. **Foster a Relocation Plan**

   Make a point by point relocation plan that frames the means, course of events, and assets expected for the change to the cloud. Focus on responsibilities in light of their criticality and intricacy. Consider directing pilot movements to approve your methodology prior to relocating strategic frameworks.

6. **Information Security and Consistence**

   Information security and consistence ought to be at the front of your cloud-first system. Carry out vigorous safety efforts to safeguard delicate information and guarantee consistence with industry guidelines. This incorporates encryption, access controls, and constant checking.

7. **Preparing and Ability Advancement**

   Cloud reception frequently requires a change in abilities and mastery inside the association. Put resources into preparing and ability advancement projects to guarantee that your IT group has the essential information to really oversee cloud assets.

8. **Screen and Advance**

When the movement is finished, lay out checking and streamlining processes. Ceaselessly screen the exhibition, cost, and security of your cloud assets. Streamline designs and asset utilization to guarantee cost-productivity and ideal execution.

Difficulties and Contemplations

1. **Security and Consistence**

   Guaranteeing the security of information and applications in the cloud is a top concern. Associations should execute vigorous safety efforts and keep up with consistence with industry guidelines. Moreover, they ought to have emergency courses of action set up for information breaks or security occurrences.

2. **Information Move and Combination**

   Moving information from on-premises conditions to the cloud can be intricate, particularly for huge datasets. Joining between cloud-put together and with respect to premises frameworks may likewise present difficulties. A thoroughly examined information system is critical for resolving these issues.

3. **Cost Administration**

   While distributed computing can offer expense reserve funds, it's fundamental to oversee cloud costs successfully. Associations ought to ceaselessly screen their cloud use and streamline asset designation to stay away from surprising costs.

4. **Merchant Lock-In**

   Merchant secure is a potential concern while depending on a particular cloud supplier's exclusive administrations. To alleviate this gamble, associations can take on multi-cloud or half breed cloud techniques to keep up with adaptability.

5. **Expertise Hole**

   Taking on cloud-first procedures frequently requires a change in quite a while and skill. Associations might have to upskill their IT groups or recruit cloud specialists to successfully oversee and upgrade cloud assets.

6. Change The executives

Progressing to a cloud-first methodology can disturb existing cycles and work processes. Viable change the executives is critical to guarantee that representatives adjust to the better approach for working and make the most of cloud capacities.

The Advancing Scene of Distributed computing

1. **Serverless Processing**

   Serverless processing abstracts away framework the executives, permitting engineers to zero in exclusively on composing code. This pattern is acquiring prevalence for its capacity to work on application advancement and diminish functional above.

2. **Edge Figuring**

   Edge figuring carries registering assets nearer to the place where information is created, decreasing inactivity and empowering on-going handling. Especially pertinent for applications require low idleness, like IoT gadgets and independent vehicles.

3. **Containerization and Kubernetes**

   Compartments and Kubernetes have changed application organization and the executives. They offer conveyability, adaptability, and robotization, making it more straightforward to oversee complex applications in the cloud.

4. **Computerized reasoning and AI**

   Cloud suppliers are progressively offering simulated intelligence and AI administrations, democratizing admittance to cutting edge investigation and prescient capacities. These administrations empower associations to get experiences from their information and drive advancement.

5. **Manageability and Green Figuring**

Maintainability is turning into a vital thought in distributed computing. Many cloud suppliers are putting resources into sustainable power and carbon offset drives to diminish their ecological effect. Associations are likewise hoping to use cloud assets productively to limit energy utilization.

2.1 Defining Cloud-First Strategies

In the always advancing scene of data innovation, the expression "cloud-first methodology" has acquired huge noticeable quality. This approach has turned into a basic idea for associations planning to bridle the force of distributed computing to accomplish their business goals. In this investigation, we will characterize cloud-first methodologies, look at their key parts, and dive into their significance in the present advanced world.

What is a Cloud-First System?

A cloud-first system is an IT approach in which an association focuses on the utilization of distributed computing answers for its innovation needs. At its center, it connotes an essential shift away from conventional on-premises foundation and applications toward cloud-based other options. The focal thought is to use cloud innovation as the essential stage for conveying administrations, applications, and foundation.

This methodology isn't just about involving the cloud for explicit capabilities; an extensive outlook drives dynamic across the whole association. It impacts how IT assets are provisioned, how programming applications are created and conveyed, and how information is put away and made due.

Key Parts of a Cloud-First Technique

1. **Cloud-First Outlook**

   At the core of a cloud-first procedure is a change in outlook. It includes seeing the cloud not as a discretionary extra but rather as the need might arise. This outlook saturates all levels of the association, from top administration to IT groups and engineers. It energizes a culture of nonstop development and transformation.

2. **Cloud Administration Models**

   Framework as a Help (IaaS): Giving virtualized figuring assets over the web, like servers, stockpiling, and systems administration.

   Stage as a Help (PaaS): Offering a turn of events and organization climate for application designers to fabricate, send, and oversee applications without stressing over framework.

   Programming as a Help (SaaS): Conveying programming applications over the web, open through internet browsers, without the requirement for establishment or support.Associations should cautiously survey which administration models line up with their objectives and necessities and coordinate them into their technique in like manner.

3. **Cloud Sending Models**

   Public Cloud: Cloud assets are claimed and worked by an outsider cloud specialist co-op and made accessible to the overall population over the web.

   Confidential Cloud: Cloud assets are committed to a solitary association and are either facilitated on-premises or by an outsider supplier. It offers more control and customization choices.

   Half breed Cloud: Consolidating both public and confidential mists to accomplish more noteworthy adaptability and information conveyability.

   Multi-Cloud: Using numerous cloud suppliers to keep away from merchant secure and profit from the qualities of various suppliers.Associations ought to painstakingly pick the organization model that lines up with their security, consistence, and versatility needs.

4. **Information The board**

   Information is a basic part of any association's tasks. A cloud-first system incorporates contemplations for information the executives, enveloping information stockpiling, reinforcement, security, and administration. It includes arriving at informed conclusions about where and how information is put away in the cloud, as well as information access and security approaches.

5. **Security and Consistence**

   Security is a central worry in cloud-first procedures. Associations should execute hearty safety efforts to safeguard their information and applications in the cloud. This incorporates measures like encryption, personality and access the board, interruption identification, and consistence with industry-explicit guidelines.

6. **Cost Administration**

   While distributed computing offers possible expense reserve funds, associations should actually deal with their cloud costs. This includes observing cloud asset use, upgrading designs, and taking on savvy valuing models, for example, pay-more only as costs arise or held occasions.

7. **Administration and Control**

Cloud-first systems additionally address administration and control viewpoints. Associations should lay out clear arrangements and rules for cloud use, including asset provisioning, access controls, and consistence checks. Executing administration structures guarantees that cloud assets are utilized in a controlled and responsible way.

Why Cloud-First Techniques Matter

1. **Dexterity and Development**

   Cloud-first procedures empower associations to quickly advance. By abstracting framework the executives, groups can zero in additional on creating and sending applications, exploring different avenues regarding novel thoughts, and answering rapidly to changing business sector requests. This dexterity is a vital driver of upper hand.

2. **Adaptability**

   Distributed computing offers uncommon versatility. Associations can undoubtedly increase assets or down in light of interest, guaranteeing that they can deal with traffic spikes and occasional varieties without overprovisioning exorbitant framework.

3. **Cost Effectiveness**

   Cloud-first techniques frequently lead to cost investment funds. Rather than making significant forthright interests in equipment, associations can use the pay-more only as costs arise model, paying just for the assets they use. This cost consistency is especially significant in financial plan arranging.

4. **Availability and Cooperation**

   Cloud-based arrangements upgrade availability and coordinated effort. They permit representatives to get to information and applications from anyplace with a web association, working with remote work and joint effort among dispersed groups.

5. **Fiasco Recuperation and Business Congruity**

   Cloud suppliers offer strong calamity recuperation and business progression arrangements. Information overt repetitiveness and reinforcement abilities guarantee that associations can rapidly recuperate from surprising interruptions.

6. **Upper hand**

A professional cloud-first system can give a critical upper hand. Associations can advance quicker, convey new highlights and administrations to clients all the more rapidly, and remain in front of rivals in quickly developing business sectors.

Challenges in Taking on Cloud-First Systems

1. **Security Concerns**

   Security stays a top worry in the cloud. Associations should carry out complete safety efforts to safeguard their information and applications from dangers. This incorporates getting network associations, carrying out access controls, and encoding delicate information.

2. **Consistence**

   Consistence with industry-explicit guidelines is a complicated test in the cloud. Associations should guarantee that their cloud organizations meet all pertinent consistence prerequisites, which frequently include severe information taking care of and stockpiling rules.

3. **Information Relocation**

   Moving existing information and applications to the cloud can be a complex and tedious cycle. Information relocation systems should think about information honesty, personal time, and the consistent progress of jobs.

4. **Cost Administration**

   While distributed computing offers cost reserve funds, associations should effectively deal with their cloud spend. Inability to do so can prompt unforeseen expense overwhelms. Nonstop checking and enhancement are fundamental.

5. **Expertise Hole**

Progressing to a cloud-first procedure might require upskilling or recruiting cloud specialists. Associations should put resources into preparing to guarantee that their IT groups have the important abilities to actually oversee cloud assets.

In the present computerized age, the reception of a cloud-first system is something beyond a pattern; it's an essential objective. It addresses a central change in how associations approach IT, stressing nimbleness, versatility, cost-productivity, and development. By embracing cloud-first procedures, organizations can situate themselves for outcome in a quickly developing mechanical scene. Notwithstanding, they should likewise address difficulties like security, consistence, information relocation, cost administration, and ability advancement to completely understand the advantages of the cloud-first methodology. Eventually, an obvious and painstakingly executed cloud-first methodology can enable associations to flourish in the computerized time.

2.2 Benefits of Adopting Cloud-First Approaches

In the present computerized age, where innovation is at the center of business tasks, taking on a cloud-first methodology has become basic for associations of all sizes and enterprises. A cloud-first procedure focuses on the utilization of distributed computing for IT needs, and its advantages stretch out a long ways past simple comfort. This article investigates the huge benefits of embracing cloud-first methodologies, going from cost reserve funds to further developed readiness and advancement.

1. **Cost Proficiency**

   One of the most convincing purposes behind taking on a cloud-first methodology is cost effectiveness. Customary on-premises foundation requires huge forthright interests in equipment, server farms, and continuous upkeep. Interestingly, distributed computing offers a pay-more only as costs arise model, where associations pay just for the assets they use. This outcomes in decreased capital consumptions, lower functional expenses, and more noteworthy expense consistency.

   Cloud suppliers ordinarily offer a scope of estimating models, permitting associations to pick the one that best lines up with their spending plan and use designs. Whether it's held occurrences for consistent responsibilities or on-request occasions for variable jobs, distributed computing gives adaptability in overseeing costs.

2. **Adaptability**

   Cloud-first methodologies empower associations to scale assets quickly in light of evolving requests. Customary foundation frequently requires significant lead time to arrangement extra servers or equipment. Conversely, cloud administrations consider moment increasing or down, guaranteeing that associations can fulfill spikes in need without overprovisioning assets.

   This versatility is especially advantageous for organizations with variable responsibilities, for example, internet business stages encountering traffic floods during occasions or retail deals occasions. It guarantees that assets are distributed productively, improving both execution and cost.

3. **Readiness and Speed**

   Readiness is a critical driver of outcome in the present speedy business climate. Cloud-first systems enable associations to be more nimble and receptive to advertise changes. With distributed computing, designers can turn up new conditions and assets rapidly, decreasing chance to-showcase for new items and highlights. Besides, cloud administrations give a stage to nonstop reconciliation and consistent sending (CI/Cd), empowering associations to mechanize and smooth out the product improvement and delivery process. This robotization prompts quicker advancement cycles, successive updates, and further developed advancement abilities.

4. **Availability and Coordinated effort**

   The cloud upgrades openness and coordinated effort for associations with remote or circulated groups. Cloud-based applications and information are available from anyplace with a web association. This availability cultivates joint effort among workers no matter what their actual area.

   Joint effort devices and stages facilitated in the cloud work with constant correspondence, document sharing, and venture the board. As remote work turns out to be more predominant, cloud-first methodologies support adaptable work plans, further develop efficiency, and guarantee business coherence.

5. **Debacle Recuperation and Business Congruity**

   Cloud-first systems intrinsically further develop catastrophe recuperation and business coherence abilities. Cloud suppliers work geologically repetitive server farms, guaranteeing that information and applications are supported and put away in various areas. This overt repetitiveness limits the gamble of information misfortune because of equipment disappointments or catastrophic events.

In case of a catastrophe, associations can rapidly recuperate their information and applications from the cloud, limiting margin time and business disturbance. This powerful catastrophe recuperation ability is in many cases more savvy and solid than customary calamity recuperation arrangements.

6. **Security and Consistence**

   Security is a main concern for associations, and cloud-first methodologies can upgrade safety efforts. Cloud suppliers put vigorously in security framework, including firewalls, encryption, access controls, and danger discovery frameworks. These implicit security highlights offer a degree of assurance that can be trying to imitate in on-premises conditions.

   Also, cloud suppliers frequently conform to industry-explicit affirmations and guidelines, which can improve on consistence endeavors for associations in directed enterprises. Cloud administrations permit associations to carry out granular access controls and screen exercises, improving their capacity to keep up with information security and meet consistence necessities.

7. **Advancement and Upper hand**

   Cloud-first methodologies let loose assets and ability to zero in on advancement as opposed to framework the executives. With distributed computing taking care of the fundamental foundation, associations can channel their endeavors into creating inventive items and administrations.

   Cloud benefits likewise give admittance to state of the art innovations, like computerized reasoning (man-made intelligence), AI, and huge information investigation, which can drive development and give an upper hand. Associations can tackle these advances without the requirement for huge forthright interests in equipment and programming.

8. **Green Figuring**

   Supportability and natural obligation are turning out to be

progressively significant contemplations for associations. Cloud suppliers are putting forth attempts to lessen their ecological effect through drives, for example, utilizing environmentally friendly power sources, streamlining server farm activities, and carrying out energy-productive innovations.

By embracing cloud-first systems, associations can in a round-about way add to green figuring endeavors. Cloud server farms are in many cases more energy-effective and harmless to the eco-system than customary on-premises server farms. This lines up with corporate social obligation objectives and can be a convincing justification for taking on cloud-first methodologies.

9. **Overt repetitiveness and High Accessibility**

Cloud suppliers offer elevated degrees of overt repetitiveness and accessibility. Information is reproduced across various server farms in various geographic areas, diminishing the gamble of information misfortune because of equipment disappointments or local blackouts. This high accessibility guarantees that applications stay open to clients, even notwithstanding unanticipated interruptions.

10. **Worldwide Reach**

Cloud-first methodologies empower associations to handily extend their worldwide arrive at more.

Cloud suppliers have server farms in different locales around the world, permitting associations to convey applications and administrations nearer to their interest groups. This decreases dormancy and further develops client encounters for clients and clients in various topographical areas.

The advantages of embracing cloud-first methodologies are multi-layered and reach out across cost proficiency, adaptability, nimbleness, security, availability, and development. As innovation keeps on propelling, associations that embrace cloud-first procedures are better situated to flourish in a quickly changing business scene.

It's vital to take note of that while cloud-first procedures offer various benefits, they likewise accompany difficulties, including security concerns, consistence contemplations, and cost administration. Fruitful reception requires cautious preparation, continuous streamlining, and a guarantee to tending to these difficulties really.

In rundown, a top notch cloud-first methodology can empower associations to lessen costs, upgrade readiness, drive development, and stay serious in the computerized period. It addresses an essential shift that can open additional opportunities and drive business outcome in reality as we know it where innovation is key to each part of tasks.

2.3 Cloud-First vs. Traditional IT Infrastructure

In the domain of IT direction, associations are confronted with a vital decision: whether with embrace a cloud-first methodology or comply to customary on-premises IT framework. This choice can have extensive ramifications for cost productivity, adaptability, nimbleness, security, and generally seriousness. In this complete examination, we will investigate the vital contrasts between cloud-first and customary IT framework and evaluate the benefits and detriments of each methodology.

Cloud-First IT Foundation

Definition

A cloud-first IT framework is a methodology where associations focus on distributed computing answers for their IT needs. Cloud-first methodologies underscore utilizing cloud administrations, stages, and foundation as the essential method for conveying innovation arrangements.

Key Qualities

Versatility: Cloud-first foundation offers quick adaptability. Associations can without much of a stretch change registering assets up or down in view of interest, guaranteeing proficient asset use.

Cost Effectiveness: Cloud-first methodologies frequently lead to cost investment funds. With a pay-more only as costs arise valuing model, associations pay just for the assets they use, wiping out the requirement for critical forthright capital consumptions.

Dexterity and Development: Cloud-first procedures advance spryness and advancement by abstracting foundation the board. Engineers can quickly create, test, and convey applications, prompting more limited improvement cycles and speedier opportunity to-showcase.

Availability and Coordinated effort: Cloud-based arrangements are open from anyplace with a web association, working with remote work and cooperation among disseminated groups.

Security and Consistence: Cloud suppliers put vigorously in security foundation, offering strong security highlights, consistence affirmations, and the capacity to carry out granular access controls.

Benefits

Cost Investment funds: Cloud-first methodologies can decrease capital consumptions and continuous functional expenses, making them more financially savvy than customary IT framework.

Versatility: Associations can scale assets on-request, guaranteeing that they satisfy vacillations in need productively without overprovisioning.

Adaptability: Cloud-first procedures give adaptability to adjust to changing economic situations and innovation patterns, permitting associations to remain cutthroat.

Advancement: By offloading framework the board to cloud suppliers, associations can zero in on advancement and item improvement.

Availability: Cloud-based arrangements improve openness and backing remote work, empowering coordinated effort among worldwide groups.

Disservices

Security Concerns: Associations might have worries about information security and control while moving to the cloud, especially for delicate or managed information.

Complex Relocation: Moving existing on-premises frameworks and information to the cloud can be mind boggling and may require cautious preparation and execution.

Cost Administration: While distributed computing offers cost reserve funds, associations should effectively deal with their cloud spend to stay away from startling costs.

Expertise Hole: Progressing to a cloud-first methodology might require upskilling or recruiting cloud specialists, which can be difficult for certain associations.

Customary IT Foundation

Definition

Conventional IT foundation alludes to on-premises figuring arrangements where associations own and deal with their equipment, server farms, and systems administration gear. In this methodology, all IT assets are actually situated inside the association's premises.

Key Qualities

Control: Customary IT foundation furnishes associations with full command over their equipment, information, and safety efforts.

Information Area: Information is put away locally on association claimed servers, giving associations direct admittance to and command over their information.

Unsurprising Expenses: Customary foundation costs are frequently unsurprising, with capital consumptions made forthright for equipment and programming.

Security Customization: Associations can execute profoundly tweaked safety efforts custom-made to their particular necessities.

Benefits

Information Control: Associations have unlimited authority over their information and can carry out unambiguous security and consistence measures.

Security: For certain associations, especially those with tough security and consistence necessities, customary foundation might offer a more elevated level of seen security.

Unsurprising Expenses: Conventional IT framework costs are unsurprising, making spending plan arranging more direct.

No Merchant Lock-In: Associations are not attached to a particular cloud supplier, which gives adaptability in picking innovation arrangements.

Drawbacks

High Beginning Expenses: Customary framework requires significant forthright interests in equipment, server farms, and progressing upkeep.

Restricted Adaptability: Scaling customary foundation can be slow and expensive, frequently requiring lead time for provisioning new equipment.

Diminished Spryness: Overseeing on-premises foundation can be tedious and may dial back improvement cycles and advancement.

Support Above: Associations are answerable for keeping up with equipment, applying refreshes, and overseeing actual framework.

Restricted Availability: Conventional IT framework may not offer similar degree of openness and coordinated effort capacities as cloud arrangements, especially for remote groups.

Similar Investigation

Cost Productivity

Cloud-First: Cloud-first methodologies by and large proposition prevalent expense proficiency. With pay-more only as costs arise estimating, associations just compensation for what they use, lessening forthright capital consumptions and giving expense consistency.

Conventional IT Foundation: Customary framework frequently includes significant forthright expenses for equipment and progressing functional costs. While costs are unsurprising, they might be higher over the long haul.

Versatility

Cloud-First: Cloud-first systems succeed in versatility, permitting associations to scale assets quickly founded on request. This dexterity guarantees proficient asset use.

Conventional IT Framework: Scaling customary foundation can be slow and exorbitant, including lead time for provisioning new equipment. It might bring about overprovisioning during top periods.

Dexterity and Development

Cloud-First: Cloud-first methodologies advance dexterity and development by abstracting framework the board. Advancement cycles are more limited, and associations can answer rapidly to showcase changes.

Customary IT Framework: Conventional foundation might block deftness because of manual administration cycles and longer improvement cycles.

Availability and Cooperation

Cloud-First: Cloud-based arrangements upgrade availability and backing cooperation among disseminated groups, making them ideal for remote work.

Customary IT Framework: Conventional foundation might restrict openness and coordinated effort, especially for remote groups.

Security and Consistence

Cloud-First: Cloud suppliers put vigorously in security foundation, offering strong security elements and consistence confirmations. In any case, associations might have worries about information security and control.

Conventional IT Framework: Customary foundation permits associations to carry out profoundly modified safety efforts yet requires committed ability and assets.

Control and Information Area

Cloud-First: Cloud-first methodologies include giving up a command over equipment and information area to cloud suppliers. Information might be put away in different geographic locales.

Conventional IT Framework: Customary foundation gives full command over equipment and information area, making it reasonable for associations with explicit information power necessities.

The decision between a cloud-first procedure and conventional IT foundation is a urgent choice that associations should make in view of their extraordinary necessities, targets, and limitations. Each approach has its own arrangement of benefits and drawbacks, and the choice ought to line up with the association's all-encompassing objectives.

Generally speaking, a crossover approach might be the most reasonable arrangement, permitting associations to use the advantages of both cloud and on-premises framework. Such a methodology empowers associations to adjust the versatility and development of the cloud with the control and security of conventional foundation.

Eventually, the choice between cloud-first and conventional IT framework ought to be driven by a far reaching evaluation of an association's requirements, considering variables like expense proficiency, versatility, nimbleness, security, consistence, and openness. No matter what the picked approach, associations ought to persistently assess their IT procedures to guarantee they stay lined up with their developing business targets and innovation scene.

Chapter 3

Cloud Service Models and Deployment Models

Distributed computing has changed the manner in which associations use and deal with their IT assets. This exhaustive investigation digs into the multifaceted subtleties of cloud administration models and organization models, examining their qualities, benefits, and genuine applications.

Cloud Administration Models

1. **Foundation as a Help (IaaS)**

   Versatility: IaaS stages offer on-request adaptability, permitting associations to increment or diminishing assets on a case by case basis.

   Control: Clients have more noteworthy command over the fundamental foundation, including working frameworks, applications, and setups.

   Cost Proficiency: IaaS kills the requirement for putting resources into actual equipment, lessening capital uses.

   Model Suppliers: Amazon Web Administrations (AWS), Microsoft Sky blue, Google Cloud Stage (GCP), and IBM Cloud.

2. **Stage as a Help (PaaS)**

   Deliberation: PaaS abstracts the fundamental framework, permitting designers to zero in exclusively on application improvement.

   Simplicity of Organization: PaaS stages smooth out application arrangement, lessening the intricacy of overseeing servers and middleware.

   Programmed Scaling: Numerous PaaS suppliers offer programmed scaling in view of traffic and asset usage.

   Model Suppliers: Heroku, Google Application Motor, Microsoft Purplish blue Application Administration, and Red Cap OpenShift.

3. **Programming as a Help (SaaS)**

   Availability: SaaS applications are open from any gadget with a web association.

   Overseen Administrations: The supplier oversees application updates, security, and framework.

   Versatility: SaaS applications can frequently scale flawlessly to oblige client development.

   Model Suppliers: Salesforce, Google Work area (previously G Suite), Microsoft Office 365, and Zoom.

4. **Capability as a Help (FaaS) or Serverless Registering**

Occasion Driven: FaaS executes capabilities because of explicit occasions, for example, HTTP demands, data set changes, or messages.

Programmed Scaling: FaaS stages naturally scale capabilities in light of approaching occasions.

Cost Proficiency: Clients are charged exclusively for the execution season of capabilities, making it practical for irregular responsibilities.

Model Suppliers: AWS Lambda, Purplish blue Capabilities, Google Cloud Capabilities, and IBM Cloud Capabilities.

Cloud Sending Models

1. **Public Cloud**
   Versatility: Public mists offer practically boundless versatility, obliging a great many jobs.
   Cost Proficiency: Clients pay for assets on a pay-more only as costs arise or membership premise, killing the requirement for enormous forthright speculations.
   Multi-Tenure: Public mists are normally multi-occupant conditions, where different associations share a similar foundation.
   Model Suppliers: AWS, Sky blue, GCP, IBM Cloud, and Prophet Cloud.

2. **Confidential Cloud**
   Control: Confidential mists offer more prominent control and customization of framework, making them appropriate for associations with explicit necessities.
   Security: Confidential mists give upgraded security and information segregation, making them ideal for touchy information and directed ventures.
   Costs: Confidential mists frequently include higher forthright capital consumptions and continuous upkeep costs.
   Model Suppliers: VMware, OpenStack, IBM Cloud Private, and Prophet Private Cloud.

3. **Half breed Cloud**
   Adaptability: Half breed mists offer the adaptability to run responsibilities in the most proper climate, whether public or private.
   Information Compactness: Information and applications can be moved among public and confidential cloud conditions flawlessly.
   Adaptability: Associations can use the versatility of public mists while keeping up with delicate information in confidential mists.
   Model Suppliers: AWS Stations, Sky blue Circular segment, Google Anthos, and Red Cap Mixture Cloud Stage.

4. **Multi-Cloud**

Merchant Freedom: Multi-cloud methodologies forestall seller secure, permitting associations to pick the best administrations from various suppliers.

Overt repetitiveness: Multi-cloud models can give overt repetitiveness and versatility against supplier explicit blackouts.

Intricacy: Overseeing and coordinating administrations from numerous suppliers can present intricacy and require particular aptitude.

Model Suppliers: Associations might utilize blends of different cloud suppliers in light of their requirements.

Use Cases for Cloud Administration Models

IaaS: Associations requiring adaptable processing assets for facilitating applications or sites can utilize IaaS to arrangement virtual machines and capacity. This model is additionally appropriate for advancement and testing conditions.

PaaS: Engineers can utilize PaaS stages to fabricate, convey, and oversee applications without stressing over framework. It's great for web and portable application improvement, Programming interface the executives, and microservices design.

SaaS: Organizations hoping to smooth out activities can involve SaaS applications for errands like client relationship the board (CRM), email and cooperation, and HR the executives.

FaaS or Serverless: Occasion driven applications, constant information handling, and IoT (Web of Things) use cases can profit from serverless registering, where code execution is set off by occasions.

Picking the Right Cloud Administration and Arrangement Model

Business Needs: Think about your association's particular prerequisites, like versatility, control, and security.

Responsibility Qualities: Various jobs might be more qualified to explicit assistance models. Survey the idea of your jobs, whether they are process serious, information escalated, or occasion driven.

Consistence Necessities: For businesses with severe consistence prerequisites (e.g., medical care or money), private or half breed cloud models might be fundamental.

Spending plan Contemplations: Assess your spending plan imperatives and decide the most practical methodology for your association.

Information Responsiveness: Decide the awareness of your information and whether it tends to be facilitated in a public cloud or on the other hand on the off chance that it requires the security and segregation of a confidential cloud.

Existing Framework: Consider your association's current IT foundation and how it very well may be coordinated with cloud administrations.

Difficulties and Contemplations

Security: Guaranteeing information security and consistence with administrative prerequisites is urgent. Associations should execute fitting safety efforts and access controls.

Cost Administration: Cloud expenses can raise on the off chance that not oversaw really. Associations ought to screen use, carry out cost-saving measures, and pick cost-proficient help models.

Information Move and Relocation: Moving information and applications to the cloud can be mind boggling and tedious. Cautious preparation and execution are fundamental to stay away from interruptions.

Seller Lock-In: Associations should be aware of merchant secure while picking cloud suppliers and administrations. Consider taking on multi-cloud or crossover techniques to alleviate this gamble.

Abilities and Preparing: Cloud advancements develop quickly, requiring IT groups to refresh their abilities consistently. Preparing and schooling are fundamental for cloud achievement.

Cloud administration models and arrangement models furnish associations with the adaptability to fit their IT foundation to their remarkable requirements. Understanding the attributes and benefits of each assistance model and organization model is essential for going with informed choices in the present powerful innovation scene.

As associations leave on their cloud processes, they should cautiously survey their prerequisites, think about responsibility qualities, and figure security and consistence contemplations. By choosing the right blend of cloud administration and sending models, associations can use the force of distributed computing to drive advancement, improve adaptability, and stay serious in the computerized period.

3.1 Exploring Cloud Service Models (IaaS, PaaS, SaaS)

Distributed computing has altered the manner in which organizations access and deal with their IT assets. At the core of distributed computing are three crucial help models: Framework as an Assistance (IaaS), Stage as a Help (PaaS), and Programming as a Help (SaaS). These models offer shifting degrees of control, adaptability, and the executives for associations looking to use the advantages of the cloud. In this investigation, we will dive into every one of these cloud administration models, looking at their qualities, benefits, and certifiable use cases.

1. Foundation as a Help (IaaS)

1.1 Definition

Foundation as a Help (IaaS) is a cloud administration model that gives virtualized registering assets over the web. It offers associations the capacity to lease principal IT foundation parts, including virtual machines, stockpiling, and systems administration, from a cloud supplier. IaaS abstracts the fundamental equipment, permitting clients to oversee and control virtualized assets depending on the situation.

1.2 Qualities

1. Versatility

IaaS stages are intended to be exceptionally versatile, empowering associations to increase assets or down in view of interest. This versatility guarantees effective asset usage, wiping out the requirement for overprovisioning and related costs.

2. **Control**

Clients of IaaS stages have a more serious level of command over the fundamental foundation. They can pick and design working frameworks, applications, and systems administration parts, giving them adaptability to fit assets to their particular requirements.

3. **Cost Effectiveness**

IaaS kills the requirement for associations to put resources into actual equipment, decreasing capital uses. Clients pay for cloud assets on a pay-more only as costs arise or membership premise, making it a practical answer for different responsibilities.

4. **Model Suppliers**

Unmistakable IaaS suppliers incorporate Amazon Web Administrations (AWS), Microsoft Purplish blue, Google Cloud Stage (GCP), and IBM Cloud.

1.3 Use Cases

Site Facilitating: Associations can have sites and web applications on virtual machines in the cloud, scaling assets on a case by case basis to oblige traffic vacillations.

Improvement and Testing: IaaS stages give savvy conditions to advancement, testing, and arranging of uses, diminishing the requirement for on-premises foundation.

Information Capacity and Reinforcement: IaaS offers versatile capacity arrangements, going with it an optimal decision for information capacity and reinforcement.

Fiasco Recuperation: Associations can utilize IaaS to establish catastrophe recuperation conditions, guaranteeing business coherence if there should be an occurrence of unforeseen blackouts.

2. Stage as a Help (PaaS)

2.1 Definition

Stage as a Help (PaaS) is a cloud administration model that gives an extensive turn of events and sending climate in the cloud. PaaS abstracts a large part of the hidden foundation, offering instruments, administrations, and systems that improve on application advancement, sending, and the executives. It permits engineers to zero in on composing code and building applications as opposed to overseeing framework.

2.2 Qualities

1. **Reflection**

   PaaS abstracts the intricacy of framework the board, empowering designers to focus exclusively on application improvement. This reflection improves on the advancement cycle and diminishes the time expected to offer applications for sale to the public.

2. **Simplicity of Organization**

   PaaS stages smooth out the organization interaction, robotizing undertakings, for example, application scaling, load adjusting, and information base administration. This works on the arrangement of uses and lessens functional above.

3. **Programmed Scaling**

   Numerous PaaS suppliers offer programmed scaling abilities, permitting applications to deal with shifting degrees of traffic and asset requests. This guarantees ideal execution and cost proficiency.

4. **Model Suppliers**

Well known PaaS suppliers incorporate Heroku, Google Application Motor, Microsoft Sky blue Application Administration, and Red Cap OpenShift.

2.3 Use Cases

Web and Versatile Application Improvement: Designers can utilize PaaS to construct web and portable applications rapidly and productively, utilizing pre-assembled administrations and structures.

Programming interface The board: PaaS stages give apparatuses to Programming interface the executives, making it more straightforward to make and oversee APIs for application mix.

Microservices Engineering: PaaS upholds the turn of events and arrangement of microservices, empowering associations to fabricate adaptable and secluded applications.

DevOps and Consistent Coordination/Ceaseless Arrangement (CI/Cd): PaaS stages work with DevOps rehearses via mechanizing application sending and reconciliation processes.

3. Programming as a Help (SaaS)

3.1 Definition

Programming as a Help (SaaS) is a cloud administration model that conveys programming applications over the web on a membership premise. With SaaS, clients can access and utilize applications straightforwardly from an internet browser without the requirement for establishment or upkeep. The product is facilitated and overseen by a cloud supplier, who is liable for updates, security, and foundation.

3.2 Qualities

1. **Availability**

   SaaS applications are available from any gadget with a web association, furnishing clients with the adaptability to work from anyplace. This openness encourages joint effort among disseminated groups.

2. **Overseen Administrations**

   SaaS suppliers deal with all parts of the product, including updates, security, and framework support. Clients can zero in on utilizing the product as opposed to agonizing over its hidden innovation.

3. **Versatility**

   SaaS applications are intended to scale flawlessly to oblige client development. Clients can frequently add or eliminate licenses on a case by case basis without significant disturbances.

4. Model Suppliers

Conspicuous SaaS suppliers incorporate Salesforce, Google Work area (previously G Suite), Microsoft Office 365, Zoom, and Dropbox.

3.3 Use Cases

Office Efficiency: Associations use SaaS for office efficiency suites, email and joint effort apparatuses, wiping out the requirement for on-premises programming establishments.

Client Relationship The board (CRM): SaaS-based CRM arrangements assist associations with overseeing client connections, deals, and advertising exercises.

HR The board: SaaS HR the executives programming smoothes out HR processes, including finance, enlistment, and representative advantages organization.

Content Administration: Content administration frameworks (CMS) conveyed as SaaS improve on site and content administration.

Video Conferencing and Correspondence: SaaS arrangements like Zoom and Microsoft Groups work with far off correspondence and cooperation.

In the realm of distributed computing, understanding the subtleties of cloud administration models is fundamental for associations looking to improve their IT assets. Each assistance model offers unmistakable benefits, permitting organizations to pick the one that adjusts best to their necessities and targets.

IaaS gives foundation adaptability and control, making it reasonable for facilitating sites, improvement and testing, and information stockpiling.

PaaS smoothes out application improvement and organization, making it ideal for web and portable application advancement, Programming interface the board, and microservices engineering.

SaaS conveys programming applications as overseen administrations, offering availability and versatility for office efficiency, CRM, HR the board, and that's just the beginning.

At last, the decision of a cloud administration model relies upon variables like the association's particular prerequisites, responsibility qualities, spending plan, and wanted degree of control. By utilizing the right cloud administration model, associations can saddle the force of the cloud to drive development, upgrade effectiveness, and remain cutthroat in the present quickly advancing computerized scene.

3.2 Understanding Deployment Models (Public, Private, Hybrid, Multi-Cloud)

The scene of distributed computing incorporates different arrangement models that characterize where and how cloud assets are made due, got to, and used. These arrangement models take care of the different necessities of associations, offering choices for security, versatility, cost-proficiency, and information the executives. In this thorough investigation, we will dive into every organization model, including Public Cloud, Confidential Cloud, Half and half Cloud, and Multi-Cloud, to acquire a more profound comprehension of their qualities, benefits, and certifiable applications.

1. Public Cloud

1.1 Definition

Public Cloud is a cloud sending model where cloud assets, including servers, stockpiling, and systems administration, are possessed and worked by an outsider cloud specialist co-op and made accessible to the overall population over the web. These assets are commonly presented on a pay-more only as costs arise or membership premise, and clients can get to and oversee them through web points of interaction or APIs.

1.2 Attributes

1. Adaptability

Public mists are intended to be profoundly adaptable, permitting associations to extend or get their cloud assets as per request. This flexibility is particularly advantageous for taking care of fluctuating responsibilities and obliging development without forthright capital speculations.

2. **Cost Proficiency**

Public cloud clients benefit from cost-proficient cloud asset the board, as they just compensation for the assets they use. This takes out the requirement for associations to put resources into and keep up with actual equipment, decreasing both forthright and progressing costs.

3. **Multi-Occupancy**

Public mists are normally multi-occupant conditions, implying that various associations share a similar cloud foundation. This multi-occupancy model empowers cloud suppliers to accomplish economies of scale, driving down costs for clients.

4. **Model Suppliers**

Noticeable public cloud suppliers incorporate Amazon Web Administrations (AWS), Microsoft Sky blue, Google Cloud Stage (GCP), IBM Cloud, and Prophet Cloud.

1.3 Use Cases

Web Application Facilitating: Associations can have web applications and sites on open cloud servers, profiting from versatility and dependability.

Improvement and Testing Conditions: Public mists give practical conditions to programming advancement, testing, and arranging.

Information Investigation and Huge Information Handling: Public cloud stages offer the registering power and capacity expected for information serious responsibilities and examination.

Content Conveyance: Public cloud suppliers offer Substance Conveyance Organization (CDN) administrations for conveying content and media effectively.

2. Confidential Cloud

2.1 Definition

Confidential Cloud is a cloud sending model where cloud assets are committed to a solitary association or business element. Dissimilar to public mists, confidential mists can be facilitated either on-premises inside an association's server farm or by an outsider supplier. The essential attribute of private mists is that they offer more prominent control, customization, and disconnection.

2.2 Attributes

1. **Control**
   Confidential mists give associations a serious level of command over their cloud foundation. Clients can tweak the climate to meet their particular necessities, including network arrangements and security approaches.

2. **Security and Information Detachment**
   Confidential mists offer improved security and information separation contrasted with public mists. Associations with delicate information or administrative consistence needs frequently pick private cloud answers for keep up with severe command over information.

3. **Cost Contemplations**
   While private mists offer control and security benefits, they commonly include higher forthright capital consumptions for equipment, as well as progressing support costs. This cost construction might make them less savvy for certain associations.

4. **Model Suppliers**

Instances of private cloud arrangements incorporate VMware vCloud, OpenStack, and cloud arrangements presented by devoted facilitating suppliers.

2.3 Use Cases

Controlled Enterprises: Associations in profoundly directed businesses, like money and medical care, may pick private mists to guarantee consistence with industry-explicit guidelines.

Information Protection: Associations with severe information security necessities or licensed innovation concerns might select confidential mists to keep up with full command over information.

Altered Conditions: Organizations that require redid network arrangements, security approaches, and asset designation frequently favor private mists.

Heritage Frameworks Combination: Associations with inheritance frameworks and applications might utilize private mists to incorporate and modernize their IT foundation.

3. Crossover Cloud

3.1 Definition

Crossover Cloud is a cloud sending model that consolidates components of both public and confidential mists. It permits information and applications to be shared and coordinated consistently among public and confidential cloud conditions. The objective of a half and half cloud is to give adaptability, permitting associations to use the qualities of both sending models.

3.2 Attributes

1. **Adaptability**

   Mixture mists offer adaptability by empowering associations to run jobs in the most proper climate. They can use the versatility of public mists while keeping up with control and security in confidential mists.

2. **Information Compactness**

   Information and applications can move unreservedly among public and confidential cloud conditions inside a half breed cloud arrangement. This works with information sharing, reinforcement, and catastrophe recuperation methodologies.

3. **Complex Administration**

   Dealing with a crossover cloud climate can be more mind boggling than dealing with a solitary sending model. It requires coordination and mix between the general population and confidential cloud parts.

4. **Model Suppliers**

Cloud suppliers like AWS, Sky blue, and GCP offer instruments and administrations for building and overseeing half breed cloud models. Also, half breed cloud arrangements can be redone utilizing different cloud the board stages.

3.3 Use Cases

Information Reinforcement and Recuperation: Associations can involve the public cloud for information reinforcement and recuperation, guaranteeing information overt repetitiveness and business congruity.

Versatility: Half and half mists permit associations to deal with top jobs by scaling assets in the public cloud while keeping up with gauge tasks in a confidential cloud.

Information Combination: Organizations with information spread across various areas and conditions can unite their information in a half breed cloud for more straightforward administration.

Consistence Needs: Associations with information power and consistence prerequisites can keep touchy information in a hidden cloud while using public cloud assets for non-delicate responsibilities.

4. Multi-Cloud

4.1 Definition

Multi-Cloud is a cloud sending model where associations use administrations from different cloud suppliers all the while. Dissimilar to half breed mists, which normally include two cloud suppliers (public and private), multi-cloud systems can envelop various cloud suppliers and administrations.

4.2 Qualities

1. **Merchant Autonomy**
   Multi-cloud methodologies keep associations from becoming

gotten into a solitary cloud supplier. They can pick the best administrations from various suppliers in light of explicit necessities.

2. **Overt repetitiveness**

Multi-cloud designs give overt repetitiveness and flexibility against supplier explicit blackouts or disturbances. On the off chance that one cloud supplier encounters personal time, responsibilities can be moved to another supplier.

3. **Intricacy**

Overseeing and coordinating administrations from different cloud suppliers can present intricacy and require particular aptitude in cloud arrangement and administration.

4. **Model Suppliers**

Multi-cloud techniques might include different blends of cloud suppliers, including AWS, Sky blue, GCP, IBM Cloud, and others.

4.3 Use Cases

Risk Relief: Associations can diminish the gamble of information misfortune and personal time by spreading jobs across numerous cloud suppliers.

Administration Enhancement: Organizations can pick the most practical and execution improved administrations from various suppliers for explicit jobs.

Geographic Reach: Multi-cloud permits associations to put jobs and information in geographic areas that line up with information residency and dormancy prerequisites.

Innovation Skepticism: Associations can remain innovation rationalist, choosing cloud benefits that best accommodated their innovation stack and application needs.

Understanding cloud arrangement models — Public Cloud, Confidential Cloud, Half breed Cloud, and Multi-Cloud — is significant for associations expecting to tackle the maximum capacity of distributed computing. Every sending model offers unmistakable attributes and benefits, empowering organizations to fit their cloud methodology to their particular necessities, security prerequisites, and spending plan requirements.

Public Cloud gives cost-proficient adaptability, making it reasonable for web facilitating, improvement, and information investigation.Confidential Cloud offers control and security, making it ideal for directed ventures, information protection concerns, and redid conditions.Half breed Cloud joins the qualities of public and confidential mists, working with adaptability, information movability, and complex responsibility the executives.Multi-Cloud empowers seller freedom, overt repetitiveness, and the advancement of administrations from different cloud suppliers.Choosing the right arrangement model relies upon an association's special prerequisites, consistence contemplations, and targets. By arriving at informed conclusions about cloud sending, organizations can accomplish improved dexterity, versatility, and seriousness in the present powerful advanced scene.

3.3 Choosing the Right Mix of Services and Deployment Models

In the consistently developing scene of data innovation, picking the right blend of cloud administrations and sending models is an essential basic for associations trying to streamline their IT foundation. This choice effects an association's proficiency, adaptability, security, and cost-adequacy. In this investigation, we will dive into the key factors that guide the determination of administrations and sending models, underlining the significance of adjusting cloud decisions to hierarchical objectives.

The Establishment: Characterizing Hierarchical Objectives

Cost Improvement: Lessening IT foundation costs, for example, equipment support and server farm costs.

Adaptability: Guaranteeing the capacity to increase assets or down to satisfy evolving needs.

Security and Consistence: Shielding delicate information and complying to industry-explicit guidelines and consistence necessities.

Nimbleness and Advancement: Speeding up opportunity to showcase for new items or administrations through deft turn of events and development.

Business Coherence: Guaranteeing continuous activities and fiasco recuperation capacities.

Worldwide Reach: Growing the association's geographic impression and arriving at new business sectors.

Merchant Autonomy: Keeping away from seller secure and keeping up with adaptability to switch suppliers.

Inheritance Joining: Coordinating and modernizing existing heritage frameworks and applications.

Contemplations for Picking Administrations

1. **Administration Models: IaaS, PaaS, and SaaS**

   IaaS: Select IaaS for more noteworthy command over framework and adaptability. Ideal for associations expecting to oversee virtual machines and capacity.

   PaaS: Pick PaaS while zeroing in on application advancement without stressing over framework the executives. Reasonable for web and versatile application improvement, microservices, and DevOps rehearses.

   SaaS: Select SaaS to lessen functional above and gain openness. Ideal for office efficiency apparatuses, CRM, HR the executives, and other programming applications.

2. **Adaptability**

   Versatility is a key thought while choosing cloud administrations. Decide if your association requires the capacity to quickly scale assets to oblige fluctuating responsibilities or whether a more static foundation does the trick.

   Versatility: For flighty or exceptionally factor responsibilities, focus on administrations that offer flexibility, permitting you to powerfully scale assets.

Fixed Assets: For responsibilities with predictable asset needs, fixed-asset administrations might be more practical.

3. **Security and Consistence**

   Security and consistence are vital, particularly for associations taking care of delicate information or working in controlled ventures. Assess the security highlights presented by cloud suppliers and their consistence affirmations. Survey whether extra safety efforts, for example, encryption and access controls, are fundamental.

4. **Geographic Reach**

   Assuming that your association has a worldwide presence or plans to extend globally, consider cloud suppliers with server farms in locales that line up with your business goals. Topographical variety can assist with lessening dormancy and further develop client encounters.

5. **Seller Autonomy**

   To keep away from seller secure and keep up with adaptability, embrace a multi-cloud or cross breed cloud technique. This approach empowers you to choose administrations from various suppliers, decreasing reliance on a solitary seller.

6. **Heritage Combination**

On the off chance that your association depends on heritage frameworks and applications, survey whether cloud administrations can work with their coordination and modernization.

Think about cloud suppliers that deal apparatuses and administrations for heritage framework movement.

Contemplations for Picking Sending Models

1. **Public Cloud**

   Public mists are financially savvy, versatile, and reasonable for a great many responsibilities. Nonetheless, they may not be the most ideal decision for associations with severe information security or administrative consistence necessities.

Use Cases: Public mists succeed in web facilitating, improvement and testing, information examination, content conveyance, and the sky is the limit from there.

2. **Confidential Cloud**

Confidential mists offer control, security, and customization however normally include higher forthright expenses. They are great for associations with touchy information or explicit organization designs.

Use Cases: Confidential mists are appropriate for directed enterprises, information protection concerns, and associations requiring custom organization designs.

3. **Half breed Cloud**

Half breed mists give adaptability by joining public and confidential cloud assets. They are significant for associations looking for a harmony among control and versatility.

Use Cases: Half and half mists are helpful for information reinforcement and recuperation, top responsibility taking care of, information union, and consistence needs.

4. **Multi-Cloud**

Multi-cloud procedures permit associations to bridle the qualities of various cloud suppliers however require cautious administration and mix.

Use Cases: Multi-cloud is beneficial for risk alleviation, administration enhancement, geographic reach, and innovation skepticism.

The Significance of Cloud Administration

Viable cloud administration is fundamental to oversee assets, control costs, and guarantee consistence with authoritative strategies and industry guidelines. Executing cloud administration rehearses, for example, cost following, asset labeling, and access control, is basic for effective cloud reception.

Developing with the Cloud

Picking the right blend of cloud administrations and organization models is definitely not a one-time choice however a continuous interaction.

As associations advance, their necessities and needs change. Occasional evaluations and acclimations to the cloud system are fundamental to guarantee arrangement with current objectives.

Choosing the ideal blend of cloud administrations and sending models is a complex yet pivotal errand that requests a profound comprehension of hierarchical goals, responsibility qualities, and innovation patterns. Associations should focus on cost streamlining, adaptability, security, and consistence while considering administration models (IaaS, PaaS, SaaS), versatility necessities, security, geographic reach, seller freedom, and heritage combination.

Cloud administration assumes a significant part in asset the executives and cost control. At long last, associations ought to perceive that cloud system isn't static; it should develop to meet changing business needs and mechanical progressions. By moving toward cloud decisions decisively and staying versatile, associations can open the maximum capacity of the cloud and gain an upper hand in the computerized scene.

Chapter 4

Cloud Security and Compliance

Distributed computing has changed the manner in which associations oversee and deal with information, offering adaptability, adaptability, and cost-productivity. Nonetheless, the shift to the cloud additionally brings new difficulties, especially in the domains of safety and consistence. In this thorough investigation, we will dig into the complexities of cloud security and consistence, examining the advancing danger scene, best practices for getting cloud conditions, and the basic job of consistence in shielding touchy information.

Prologue to Cloud Security and Consistence

Distributed computing has turned into a necessary piece of present day business tasks. It offers a wide exhibit of advantages, including cost reserve funds, versatility, and dexterity. Notwithstanding, these benefits accompany a huge obligation: guaranteeing the security and consistence of information put away and handled in the cloud.

The Significance of Cloud Security

Cloud security is the act of safeguarding information, applications, and framework in distributed computing conditions. It envelops an expansive range of innovations, strategies, and best practices intended to protect cloud-based resources from dangers and weaknesses. The meaning of cloud security couldn't possibly be more significant, given the delicate idea of the information frequently facilitated in the cloud.

The Job of Consistence

Notwithstanding security, consistence is one more fundamental part of overseeing information in the cloud. Consistence includes complying with explicit regulations, guidelines, and industry norms that administer how information ought to be taken care of, put away, and secured. Consistence is essential for associations working in profoundly controlled businesses like money, medical services, and government.

The Developing Danger Scene

As associations progressively depend on the cloud for their information stockpiling and handling needs, the danger scene has developed. Cybercriminals and pernicious entertainers are ceaselessly growing new strategies to think twice about conditions. Understanding these dangers is the most important phase in laying out powerful cloud safety efforts.

Normal Cloud Dangers

Information Breaks: Unapproved admittance to delicate information is a huge concern. Information breaks can result from feeble verification, misconfigured access controls, or insider dangers.

Phishing Assaults: Phishing assaults are a predominant danger wherein aggressors utilize misleading messages or sites to fool people into uncovering delicate data, for example, login certifications.

Malware: Malware, including ransomware and infections, can contaminate cloud-based frameworks and compromise information honesty.

Insider Dangers: Workers or people with admittance to an association's cloud assets can deliberately or inadvertently hurt by misusing information or taking advantage of weaknesses.

Dispersed Refusal of Administration (DDoS) Assaults: DDoS assaults can disturb cloud administrations by overpowering them with traffic, delivering them inaccessible to clients.

Information Misfortune: Information misfortune can happen because of unintentional erasures, equipment disappointments, or programming mistakes, underscoring the requirement for strong reinforcement and recuperation procedures.

Misconfigured Cloud Assets: Inadequately designed cloud assets, for example, open capacity pails or unstable information bases, can open delicate information to the public web.

Groundworks of Cloud Security

Personality and Access The board (IAM)

Solid Validation: Execute multifaceted verification (MFA) to add an additional layer of safety past usernames and passwords.

Job Based Admittance Control (RBAC): Relegate jobs and consents in view of occupation capabilities, restricting admittance to what is fundamental.

Consistent Observing: Screen client exercises and set up alarms for dubious way of behaving.

Information Encryption

Information Encryption Very still: Encode information put away in cloud data sets, record capacity, and reinforcements.

Information Encryption On the way: Use encryption conventions like SSL/TLS to safeguard information as it goes among clients and cloud administrations.

Key Administration: Carry out hearty key administration practices to protect encryption keys.

Network Security

Firewalls: Design firewalls to channel approaching and active traffic, obstructing unapproved access.

Network Division: Fragment organizations to confine delicate information and cutoff parallel development for aggressors.

Interruption Discovery and Anticipation Frameworks (IDPS): Use IDPS to recognize and answer dubious organization exercises.

Weakness The board

Standard Filtering: Direct ordinary weakness sweeps to distinguish possible shortcomings.

Fix The executives: Apply security fixes and updates speedily to relieve weaknesses.

Infiltration Testing: Perform entrance testing to reproduce true assaults and survey security controls.

Episode Reaction and Recuperation

Occurrence Discovery: Utilize devices and cycles to immediately distinguish security episodes.

Occurrence Regulation: Segregate impacted frameworks to forestall further harm.

Occurrence Recuperation: Reestablish impacted frameworks and information to ordinary activities.

Post-Episode Examination: Direct post-occurrence investigation to figure out the reason and further develop safety efforts.

Cloud Consistence

HIPAA (Medical coverage Versatility and Responsibility Act): Applies to medical services associations, safeguarding the protection and security of patient information.

PCI DSS (Installment Card Industry Information Security Standard): Relates to organizations that handle Visa installments, shielding cardholder information.

GDPR (General Information Security Guideline): Oversees the insurance of individual information for European Association (EU) residents, paying little mind to where the information is handled.

SOC 2 (Administration Association Control 2): Spotlights on security, accessibility, handling respectability, secrecy, and protection of client information.

FedRAMP (Government Hazard and Approval The board Program): Applies to cloud specialist co-ops serving U.S. government organizations.

Best Practices for Cloud Security and Consistence

Lead Normal Security Reviews and Evaluations

Consistently survey your cloud climate's security act by leading reviews, weakness appraisals, and infiltration testing. Recognize and remediate security shortcomings speedily.

Carry out Access Controls and IAM Strategies

Use IAM arrangements and access controls to guarantee that clients and applications have the fitting degree of access. Carry out RBAC to restrict access in view of occupation jobs.

Encode Delicate Information

Execute encryption for information very still and on the way. Guarantee that encryption keys are overseen safely, and utilize solid encryption calculations.

Lay out an Episode Reaction Plan

Make a complete occurrence reaction plan that frames how to recognize, answer, and recuperate from security episodes. Test the arrangement through reenactments and drills.

Train and Teach Staff

Give online protection preparing and mindfulness projects to teach representatives about security best works on, including how to perceive phishing endeavors and different dangers.

Consistently Update and Fix Frameworks

Keep all cloud assets, including virtual machines and compartments, fully informed regarding security fixes and updates to moderate weaknesses.

Screen for Inconsistencies

Carry out nonstop observing to distinguish and answer uncommon exercises or ways of behaving that might show a security occurrence.

Influence Cloud Security Administrations

Cloud suppliers offer security administrations and apparatuses that can upgrade your security pose. Use administrations like AWS Guard-Duty, Sky blue Security Community, and Google Cloud Security War room.

Record and Keep up with Consistence

Record all security and consistence related exercises, including reviews, evaluations, and security approaches. Keep up with consistence with industry-explicit guidelines and guidelines.

Reinforcement and Catastrophe Recuperation

Carry out ordinary information reinforcements and test catastrophe recuperation intends to guarantee information accessibility and business progression in case of a security occurrence.

Cloud security and consistence are vital contemplations for associations working in the computerized age. The developing danger scene requires a proactive way to deal with shielding delicate information put away and handled in cloud conditions. By carrying out prescribed procedures, directing ordinary appraisals, and remaining informed about arising dangers, associations can certainly tackle the advantages of distributed computing while at the same time safeguarding their significant resources and keeping up with consistence with industry guidelines.

4.1 Data Privacy and Security Concerns in India

India is encountering quick digitization and is one of the world's biggest buyers of internet providers and innovation. With a developing computerized economy, the nation has seen a flood in information age, stockpiling, and transmission. While this advanced change has achieved various advantages, it has likewise raised huge worries with respect to information protection and security. In this article, we will investigate the key information protection and security worries in India, the lawful system administering information assurance, and the difficulties looked in resolving these issues.

Information Protection Concerns

1. **Absence of Thorough Information Protection Regulations**
   One of the essential worries in India is the shortfall of a thorough information protection regulation as of not long ago. While the nation has had a few area explicit guidelines and rules, for example, the Data Innovation Act, 2000, and the IT (Sensible Security Practices and Methodology and Delicate Individual Information

or Data) Rules, 2011, there was no overall regulation to safeguard people's very own information across all areas.

2. **Information Breaks and Cyberattacks**

   India has seen a developing number of information breaks and cyberattacks as of late. These occurrences have uncovered delicate individual and monetary data of people, prompting data fraud, monetary extortion, and protection infringement. High-profile information breaks have impacted associations across different areas, including banking, medical care, and internet business.

3. **Absence of Information Limitation**

   Information limitation alludes to the act of putting away information inside a particular geographic locale or purview. India has considered carrying out information confinement approaches to guarantee that delicate information of Indian residents is put away inside the country. Notwithstanding, this has raised worries about consistence challenges for worldwide organizations and potential exchange boundaries.

4. **Aadhaar Security Concerns**

   The Aadhaar framework, India's remarkable distinguishing proof venture, has been a subject of debate with respect to information protection.

   While Aadhaar has smoothed out taxpayer supported organizations and further developed effectiveness, concerns have emerged about the security and abuse of Aadhaar information. The High Court of India has passed decisions to address a portion of these worries, underscoring the need to protect residents' security.

5. **Observation and Information Access**

There have been worries about government observation and the potential for unapproved admittance to individual information. The utilization of reconnaissance innovation for policing public safety purposes has prompted banters about the harmony among protection and security.

Information Security Concerns

1. **Network safety Dangers**

   India faces a consistent danger from cyberattacks, including malware, ransomware, phishing, and Circulated Refusal of Administration (DDoS) assaults. These dangers target government offices, confidential undertakings, and people, prompting information breaks and monetary misfortunes.

2. **Insider Dangers**

   Insider dangers, frequently from representatives or believed people, represent a critical security risk. Information breaks brought about by insider dangers can be deliberate, like information burglary, or unexpected, similar to inadvertent information openness.

3. **Weak IoT Gadgets**

   The expansion of Web of Things (IoT) gadgets in India has presented new security challenges. Numerous IoT gadgets need powerful security highlights, making them helpless against abuse by cybercriminals. These gadgets might possibly think twice about information and security.

4. **Outsider Information Sharing**

   Numerous associations in India team up with outsider sellers and specialist co-ops, prompting information sharing and move. Guaranteeing the security and protection of information when imparted to outside parties is a perplexing test, especially without severe guidelines.

5. **Insufficient Information Security Measures**

A few associations in India might not have executed sufficient information security measures, allowing information to remain uncovered to breaks and unapproved access. The absence of mindfulness and assets for online protection practices can add to this issue.

Legitimate Structure and Information Security Guidelines

1. **The Individual Information Insurance Bill, 2019**
   The Individual Information Security Bill, 2019, means to control the handling of individual information in India. It frames standards for the assortment, stockpiling, and handling of individual information, including the arrangement of an Information Security Official (DPO) by specific information processors. The bill likewise incorporates arrangements for the exchange of individual information outside India, giving people more command over their information.

2. **The Data Innovation Act, 2000**
   The Data Innovation Act, 2000, was one of the early regulations that resolved issues connected with information assurance and network protection. It incorporates arrangements for the discipline of cybercrimes and the foundation of the Indian PC Crisis Reaction Group (CERT-In) for answering network safety episodes.

3. **Aadhaar Act, 2016**
   The Aadhaar Act, 2016, administers the utilization of the Aadhaar framework for ID purposes. While it has been reprimanded for security concerns, the High Court of India has maintained its lawfulness while stressing the need to safeguard residents' protection.

4. **Area Explicit Guidelines**

Certain areas, like banking and medical care, have their own area explicit guidelines and rules for information security. For instance, the Save Bank of India (RBI) has given online protection rules for banks and monetary organizations.

Difficulties and Future Bearings

1. **Requirement and Execution**
   Successful requirement of information security regulations and

guidelines stays a test. Fostering the essential framework and assets for upholding these regulations is basic to their prosperity.

2. **Information Limitation**

   The discussion over information limitation proceeds, with worries about its effect on cross-line information streams, worldwide exchange, and consistence for global organizations.

3. **Mindfulness and Instruction**

   Bringing issues to light about information protection and security among people and associations is fundamental. Numerous information breaks happen because of human blunder or absence of mindfulness.

4. **Network protection Readiness**

   Building powerful online protection abilities and readiness is urgent to guarding against digital dangers. This remembers speculation for innovation, preparing, and occurrence reaction.

5. **Adjusting Protection and Security**

Finding the right harmony among protection and security is a continuous test. Finding some kind of harmony requires cautious thought of individual privileges and public safety interests.

4.2 Regulatory Landscape (Data Localization, Data Sovereignty)

The administrative scene overseeing information restriction and information sway has become progressively perplexing and significant in the present interconnected computerized world. As information streams across borders effortlessly, legislatures and associations wrestle with the need to safeguard delicate information, guarantee security, and declare ward over advanced resources. In this investigation, we will dig into the ideas of information limitation and information sway, their importance, the purposes for their reception, and their effect on organizations and people.

Information Limitation: Characterizing the Idea

Information limitation, otherwise called information residency or information training, alludes to the act of expecting information to be put away and handled inside a particular geographic area or purview. Generally, it confines the development of information across public boundaries and commands that information should be truly housed inside the lines of a specific nation or locale. Information confinement guidelines can cover different kinds of information, including individual data, monetary records, and touchy corporate information.

Information Sway: Grasping the Guideline

Information sway is a connected idea that spotlights on the declaration of lawful ward and command over information. It infers that information is dependent upon the regulations and guidelines of the nation or district where it is found or where the information's proprietor dwells. Information power is frequently connected to information confinement prerequisites, as the last option is a method for implementing information sway.

Purposes behind Information Restriction and Information Sway

1. **Information Security and Assurance**

   One of the essential purposes behind information confinement is to improve information security and assurance. State run administrations look to guarantee that delicate information, like individual data and monetary records, is put away and handled inside their locale to defend the privileges and protection of their residents.

2. **Public safety**

   Public safety concerns likewise assume a huge part in information confinement. State run administrations might need to keep up with command over specific information, especially basic foundation and safeguard related data, to safeguard against digital dangers and secret activities.

3. **Administrative Consistence**

   Numerous nations have authorized information security and protection regulations that expect associations to consent to explicit information dealing with and capacity guidelines. Information confinement guarantees that associations comply with these regulations by keeping information inside the ward where the guidelines apply.

4. **Financial Interests**

   Information limitation can be spurred by monetary interests, for example, advancing nearby server farm framework, making position, and sustaining the development of the homegrown innovation area.

5. **Social and Social Qualities**

A few countries might take on information restriction necessities to maintain social and social qualities. For example, certain nations might need to safeguard their social legacy and protected innovation by declaring command over information connected with these angles.

Influence on Organizations and People

1. **Consistence Difficulties**

   Organizations that work globally face huge consistence challenges. They should explore a perplexing snare of information insurance regulations and restriction necessities, which might change starting with one country then onto the next. This can prompt expanded consistence costs and authoritative weights.

2. **Influence on Cross-Boundary Information Streams**

   Information limitation measures can upset the progression of information across borders. This can influence organizations that depend on distributed computing, worldwide information organizations, and global coordinated efforts. It might likewise bring about more slow information move speeds and expanded inertness.

3. **Cost Contemplations**

   Keeping up with server farms and framework inside unambiguous wards can be expensive for organizations. These expenses can incorporate development costs, continuous support, and consistence endeavors.

4. **Information Access and Accessibility**

   Information limitation might influence information access and accessibility. People and organizations might confront difficulties getting to their information while voyaging or directing worldwide business. Furthermore, information put away inside a particular purview might be dependent upon government access demands, possibly influencing information protection.

5. **Advancement and Rivalry**

Information restriction can influence development and contest inside the innovation area. It might deter unfamiliar innovation organizations from entering specific business sectors, restricting contest and possibly smothering advancement.

Worldwide Varieties in Information Restriction and Information Sway

1. **European Association (EU)**

   The EU's Overall Information Security Guideline (GDPR) accentuates information insurance and protection.

   While it doesn't command information restriction, it puts severe prerequisites on the exchange of individual information outside the EU, requiring measures like Standard Authoritative Conditions (SCCs) and Restricting Corporate Guidelines (BCRs) for worldwide information moves.

2. **China**

   China has quite possibly of the most thorough datum restriction systems on the planet. The country's Network protection Regulation requires the capacity of "basic information" and individual data of Chinese residents inside China. This guideline has critical ramifications for global organizations working in China.

3. **Russia**

Russia's information confinement regulation, known as the "Russian Information Restriction Regulation," orders that individual information of Russian residents should be put away and handled on servers actually situated inside the country. Inability to agree can bring about fines and limitations on information handling.

4. **US**

The US doesn't have government information limitation regulations. In any case, a few states have ordered information break notice regulations and information security guidelines that might apply to specific businesses and circumstances.

4.3 Cloud Security Best Practices

Distributed computing has altered the manner in which associations work, offering versatility, adaptability, and cost-productivity. Notwithstanding, with the advantages of the cloud come security difficulties and obligations. As associations move to the cloud, it's crucial for carry out strong cloud security practices to safeguard delicate information, keep up with consistence, and moderate online protection gambles. In this aide, we will investigate cloud security best practices that can assist you with protecting your advanced resources in the cloud.

Comprehend the Common Obligation Model

Cloud suppliers follow a common obligation model, and that truly intends that while they secure the basic foundation, clients are liable for getting their information and applications inside the cloud. It's pivotal to comprehend this model and your obligations inside it to guarantee extensive security.

Foundation Security: Cloud suppliers, like AWS, Sky blue, and Google Cloud, are answerable for getting the actual server farms, network framework, and hypervisors.

Client Security: Clients are answerable for getting their information, applications, character and access the board, network designs, and consistence with administrative necessities.

Execute Solid Character and Access The board (IAM)

Multifaceted Confirmation (MFA): Require MFA for all client records to add an additional layer of safety past passwords.

Job Based Admittance Control (RBAC): Appoint consents in view of occupation jobs, restricting admittance to what's essential.

Least Honor Guideline: Award the base degree of access expected for clients to play out their errands.

Standard Audit and Cleanup: Occasionally survey and renounce pointless access honors to limit the assault surface.

Secure Your Information with Encryption

Information encryption is basic to shield delicate data from unapproved access, both on the way and very still.

Information Encryption Very still: Encode information put away in data sets, record capacity, and reinforcements. Use encryption keys and oversee them safely.

Information Encryption On the way: Use encryption conventions like SSL/TLS to safeguard information as it goes among clients and cloud administrations.

Design Organization Security

Legitimate organization security is fundamental to forestall unapproved access and safeguard your cloud assets.

Virtual Confidential Cloud (VPC) or Virtual Organization (VNet): Utilize these organization separation instruments to fragment assets and control traffic stream.

Firewalls: Design firewalls to channel approaching and active traffic, impeding unapproved access.

Network Security Gatherings (NSGs): Use NSGs to characterize inbound and outbound security rules for assets inside your VPC or VNet.

Interruption Location and Avoidance Frameworks (IDPS): Utilize IDPS to recognize and answer dubious organization exercises.

Screen and Review Action

Persistent checking and evaluating help you identify and answer security episodes continuously.

Cloud Checking Administrations: Use cloud supplier explicit observing administrations, like AWS CloudWatch, Purplish blue Screen, or Google Cloud Checking, to gather and examine information about your assets' exhibition and security.

Log Assortment and Investigation: Unify and dissect logs from different cloud administrations to recognize security dangers and oddities.

Security Data and Occasion The executives (SIEM): Carry out a SIEM framework to correspond security occasions and computerize episode reaction.

Lay out an Episode Reaction Plan

Episode Recognition: Utilize instruments and cycles to quickly recognize security occurrences.

Occurrence Regulation: Separate impacted frameworks to forestall further harm.

Episode Recuperation: Reestablish impacted frameworks and information to ordinary activities.

Post-Episode Investigation: Lead present occurrence examination on grasp the reason and further develop safety efforts.

Execute Security Best Practices for Holders and Serverless Registering

Compartment Security: Use holder security devices and practices, for example, picture examining, runtime assurance, and compartment explicit IAM jobs.

Serverless Security: Follow best practices for serverless security, including getting capability code, utilizing fine-grained IAM consents, and checking for dubious action.

Routinely Update and Fix Frameworks

Staying up with the latest with security fixes and updates is imperative to alleviate weaknesses. Execute a viable fix the executives procedure to guarantee all frameworks are current.

Reinforcement and Calamity Recuperation

Carry out customary information reinforcements and test debacle recuperation intends to guarantee information accessibility and business congruity in case of a security occurrence.

Lead Security Preparing and Mindfulness

Teach your workers about security best works on, including how to perceive phishing endeavors and different dangers. Guarantee that your staff knows about the association's security arrangements and systems.

Consistence and Administration

Keep up with consistence with industry-explicit principles and guidelines. Execute cloud administration rehearses, for example, cost following, asset labeling, and access control, to oversee assets and control costs really.

Merchant Appraisal

Assuming that you're utilizing outsider cloud administrations or arrangements, survey their safety efforts and guarantee they line up with your association's necessities and guidelines.

Team up with Security Specialists

Consider cooperating with experienced online protection firms or advisors to lead security evaluations, infiltration testing, and weakness appraisals to distinguish and address possible shortcomings.

Cloud security is a common obligation between cloud suppliers and clients. By following these prescribed procedures and staying careful, associations can upgrade their cloud security pose, safeguard delicate information, and decrease the gamble of safety breaks. Standard evaluations and a proactive way to deal with security are fundamental in the present developing danger scene.

4.4 Compliance and Certification Considerations

Consistence and confirmation assume an essential part in guaranteeing the security, protection, and dependability of distributed computing administrations. Associations that utilization cloud administrations should stick to administrative prerequisites, industry norms, and best practices to safeguard delicate information, keep up with client trust, and stay away from legitimate and monetary repercussions. In this article, we will investigate the significance of consistence and affirmation in distributed computing and feature key contemplations for associations trying to explore this perplexing scene.

The Meaning of Consistence and Affirmation

1. **Legitimate Commitments**
   Consistence with pertinent regulations and guidelines is an essential necessity for any association. With regards to distributed computing, fundamental to comprehend the legitimate commitments relate to the taking care of, stockpiling, and handling of information. Rebelliousness can prompt extreme punishments and lawful outcomes.

2. **Information Security and Protection**
   Safeguarding the security of people's information is a principal concern, and guidelines like the Overall Information Security Guideline (GDPR) in the European Association and the Medical coverage Convenientce and Responsibility Act (HIPAA) in the US set severe norms for information insurance. Consistence guarantees that individual and delicate information is dealt with properly.

3. **Trust and Notoriety**
   Consistence and certificate exhibit a pledge to security and protection, building entrust with clients, accomplices, and partners. Associations that can demonstrate they satisfy laid out guidelines are bound to procure and hold the trust of their clients.

4. **Risk Relief**
   Consistence estimates help distinguish and moderate security gambles, decreasing the probability of information breaks, cyberattacks, and other security occurrences. Associations that

proactively address potential dangers are more ready to actually answer dangers.

5. **Upper hand**

Certificates and consistence adherence can give an upper hand. Numerous clients focus on security and protection while picking cloud specialist organizations, making it an important selling point for organizations.

Consistence Structures and Guidelines

1. **General Information Insurance Guideline (GDPR)**
   The GDPR is a complete information insurance guideline that applies to associations taking care of the individual information of people inside the European Association (EU). It forces severe prerequisites on information handling, security, assent, and notice of information breaks.

2. **Health care coverage Convenientce and Responsibility Act (HIPAA)**
   HIPAA applies to medical services associations and oversees the treatment of safeguarded wellbeing data (PHI). Cloud suppliers and their clients should guarantee consistence while dealing with medical services information.

3. **Installment Card Industry Information Security Standard (PCI DSS)**
   PCI DSS applies to associations that handle Mastercard installments and commands security controls to safeguard cardholder information. Cloud suppliers should conform to PCI DSS necessities while taking care of installment information.

4. **Government Hazard and Approval The board Program (FedRAMP)**
   FedRAMP is a U.S. taxpayer supported initiative that normalizes security appraisals of cloud items and administrations utilized

by government organizations. Cloud suppliers looking to serve government clients should get FedRAMP approval.

5. **Public Foundation of Guidelines and Innovation (NIST) Network protection System**

   NIST offers a network safety structure that gives rules to further developing online protection risk the executives. It is generally involved by associations as a best practice.

6. **ISO/IEC 27001**

ISO/IEC 27001 is a worldwide norm for data security the executives frameworks. Associations can look for certificate to exhibit their obligation to data security.

Key Contemplations for Consistence and Certificate in Distributed computing

1. **Grasp Materialness**

   Figure out which consistence systems and guidelines are pertinent to your association in view of variables like industry, geology, and the kind of information you handle. Not all guidelines apply generally, so center around those that straightforwardly influence your activities.

2. **Evaluate Cloud Specialist organization Abilities**

   In the event that you're utilizing a cloud specialist organization, assess their consistence confirmations and safety efforts. Guarantee that they satisfy the expected guidelines and have the fundamental affirmations to help your consistence endeavors.

3. **Information Arrangement and Taking care of**

   Arrange your information to figure out its responsiveness and administrative ramifications. Carry out information taking care of approaches and methods to guarantee consistence with information assurance and protection prerequisites.

4. **Security Controls**

   Execute security controls and measures to safeguard information and frameworks. This incorporates access controls, encryption, interruption location, and occurrence reaction capacities.

5. **Information Maintenance and Erasure**

   Lay out information maintenance and cancellation arrangements to guarantee that information isn't held longer than needed. Consistence frequently expects associations to erase information when it is not generally required for its planned reason.

6. **Episode Reaction Plan**

   Foster an episode reaction plan that frames techniques for distinguishing, detailing, and relieving security occurrences. Consistently test and update this intend to guarantee its adequacy.

7. **Representative Preparation and Mindfulness**

   Teach representatives about consistence necessities, security best practices, and their part in keeping up with consistence. Ordinary preparation and mindfulness programs are fundamental.

8. **Outsider Evaluations**

   In the event that utilizing outsider administrations or merchants, evaluate their consistence with applicable guidelines and systems. Guarantee that their practices line up with your association's consistence objectives.

9. **Persistent Checking and Reviewing**

   Carry out consistent observing and evaluating cycles to recognize and answer security occurrences, survey consistence, and distinguish regions for development.

10. **Documentation and Record-Keeping**

Keep up with exhaustive documentation of your consistence endeavors, including strategies, methodology, review trails, and certificates. This documentation is fundamental for exhibiting consistence to examiners and controllers.

Consistence and affirmation contemplations are indispensable to distributed computing, as they assist associations with meeting lawful commitments, safeguard information, fabricate trust, and diminish security gambles. By figuring out the pertinent guidelines, executing vigorous safety efforts, and encouraging a culture of consistence, associations can explore the perplexing consistence scene and guarantee the respectability and security of their cloud-based tasks.

Chapter 5

Hybrid and Multi-Cloud Strategies

In the present quickly developing computerized scene, organizations are progressively going to distributed computing to drive advancement, improve adaptability, and lessen functional expenses. Two noticeable methodologies in cloud reception are Half and half Cloud and Multi-Cloud systems. These systems offer particular benefits and difficulties, and understanding their subtleties is urgent for associations trying to upgrade their cloud surroundings. This exhaustive investigation digs into the ideas, advantages, difficulties, and best practices related with Half breed and Multi-Cloud techniques.

1. Grasping Half and half Cloud

1.1. Meaning of Half breed Cloud

Half breed Cloud is a distributed computing model that consolidates on-premises foundation or confidential cloud with at least one public cloud suppliers. It offers an extension between the capacities of private and public mists, permitting associations to use the qualities of both.

1.2. Advantages of Cross breed Cloud

1.2.1. Versatility and Adaptability

Cross breed Cloud gives the adaptability to rapidly increase assets or down. Associations can deal with top responsibilities by taking advantage of public cloud assets while keeping delicate information and basic jobs on-premises.

1.2.2. Cost Improvement

By using on-premises assets for unsurprising jobs and public cloud for variable responsibilities, organizations can streamline costs, staying away from overprovisioning while at the same time profiting from pay-more only as costs arise estimating models.

1.2.3. Information Security and Consistence

Half breed Cloud permits associations to keep up with command over delicate information and follow administrative prerequisites by keeping specific information on hidden framework.

1.2.4. Fiasco Recuperation and Business Congruity

Mixture Cloud empowers vigorous fiasco recuperation arrangements, with information replication and reinforcement techniques that range both private and public mists, guaranteeing business coherence if there should arise an occurrence of unexpected occasions.

1.3. Difficulties of Crossover Cloud

1.3.1. Intricacy

Overseeing assets across numerous conditions can be intricate, requiring particular abilities and apparatuses to guarantee consistent incorporation and coordination.

1.3.2. Information Combination

Incorporating information between on-premises and cloud conditions can present difficulties, particularly while managing dissimilar information sources and organizations.

1.3.3. Security Concerns

Getting information and applications across cross breed conditions requests a thorough methodology, including character and access the executives, encryption, and organization security.

1.3.4. Seller Lock-In

Crossover Cloud can present merchant secure on the off chance that associations depend too vigorously on a particular cloud supplier's administrations or innovations.

2. Embracing Multi-Cloud Systems

2.1. Meaning of Multi-Cloud

Multi-Cloud is a methodology that includes utilizing different cloud suppliers to meet explicit business needs. Not at all like Mixture Cloud, Multi-Cloud doesn't be guaranteed to include on-premises foundation; all things considered, it centers around utilizing different public cloud stages.

2.2. Advantages of Multi-Cloud

2.2.1. Merchant Variety

Multi-Cloud gives associations the opportunity to pick the best-fit cloud administrations from different suppliers, keeping away from merchant secure and advancing solid contest.

2.2.2. High Accessibility

Conveying responsibilities across various cloud suppliers guarantees high accessibility and lessens the gamble of administration disturbances because of blackouts or different issues.

2.2.3. Geographic Reach

Multi-Cloud empowers organizations to convey assets in server farms situated in various areas, further developing dormancy and giving better client encounters to worldwide clients.

2.2.4. Cost Enhancement

By choosing financially savvy administrations from various suppliers, associations can improve their cloud spending and try not to overpay for assets.

2.3. Difficulties of Multi-Cloud

2.3.1. Intricacy and Coordination

Overseeing and coordinating assets and administrations across different cloud suppliers can be perplexing, requiring strong administration and arrangement arrangements.

2.3.2. Expertise Necessities

Multi-Cloud conditions request a different arrangement of abilities and mastery to oversee different cloud stages and their extraordinary administrations really.

2.3.3. Security and Consistence

Guaranteeing steady security and consistence across different cloud suppliers can challenge, as each might have its own security approaches and controls.

2.3.4. Cost Administration

Without legitimate expense checking and administration, Multi-Cloud can prompt startling expense accelerations and asset spread.

3. Picking the Right Procedure

3.1. Factors Impacting Procedure Determination

3.1.1. Business Goals

The decision between Half and half Cloud and Multi-Cloud ought to line up with the association's particular objectives and prerequisites, for example, versatility, information control, and geographic reach.

3.1.2. Existing Foundation

Associations with critical on-premises speculations might incline towards Crossover Cloud, while those with a cloud-local methodology might favor Multi-Cloud.

3.1.3. Administrative Consistence

Businesses with severe information protection and consistence prerequisites might find Cross breed Cloud more reasonable because of the expanded control it offers over information.

3.1.4. Cost Contemplations

Spending plan limitations and cost advancement objectives will impact the choice among Half and half and Multi-Cloud procedures.

3.2. Carrying out a Crossover or Multi-Cloud Procedure

3.2.1. Appraisal and Arranging

Completely survey the ongoing IT scene, including applications, information, and jobs, to decide the best methodology. Foster a reasonable movement and organization plan.

3.2.2. Foundation as Code (IaC)

Take on Framework as Code practices to mechanize the provisioning and the board of assets, guaranteeing consistency and decreasing manual blunders.

3.2.3. Cloud The executives and Coordination

Put resources into cloud the executives and coordination devices that give perceivability, administration, and robotization abilities across cross breed or multi-cloud conditions.

3.2.4. Security and Consistence

Carry out a vigorous security system that incorporates personality the executives, encryption, and consistence controls custom-made to the picked technique.

3.2.5. Cost Administration

Execute cost checking and enhancement practices to forestall surprising costs and guarantee productive asset usage.

Certifiable Use Cases

4.1. Mixture Cloud Use Cases

4.1.1. Medical services

Medical services associations utilize Mixture Cloud to store patient information on-premises while utilizing the versatility of public cloud for information investigation and exploration safely.

4.1.2. Finance

Monetary foundations use Half breed Cloud for delicate monetary exchanges, keeping basic information on hidden framework while involving the public cloud for non-touchy responsibilities.

4.1.3. Retail

Retail organizations send Cross breed Cloud to deal with top shopping seasons, consistently scaling their web based business stages utilizing public cloud assets.

4.2. Multi-Cloud Use Cases

4.2.1. Internet business

Internet business organizations influence Multi-Cloud to disperse their web applications and content conveyance all around the world, guaranteeing low inertness and high accessibility.

4.2.2. Gaming

Gaming organizations send Multi-Cloud to furnish multiplayer gaming encounters with low idleness, using different cloud suppliers' server farm areas.

4.2.3. DevOps and Improvement

Associations zeroed in on DevOps and programming improvement use Multi-Cloud to get to an extensive variety of improvement apparatuses and administrations from various cloud suppliers.

5. Best Practices and Contemplations

5.1. Merchant Free-thought

Focus on merchant freethinker arrangements and structures to limit seller secure and keep up with adaptability.

5.2. Robotization

Influence robotization to smooth out asset provisioning, scaling, and the executives across half and half or multi-cloud conditions.

5.3. Observing and Investigation

Execute far reaching observing and examination devices to acquire bits of knowledge into asset execution, security, and cost.

5.4. Ability Improvement

Put resources into preparing and upskilling your IT group to oversee half breed or multi-cloud conditions successfully.

5.5. Administration and Consistence

Lay out administration structures and arrangements that address security, consistence, and information the board in accordance with the picked system.

6. Future Patterns and Difficulties

6.1. Edge Processing Coordination

The coordination of edge figuring with Cross breed and Multi-Cloud systems will turn out to be progressively significant as associations look to handle information nearer to the source.

6.2. Man-made reasoning and AI

The utilization of man-made intelligence and ML in cloud the executives and streamlining will keep on developing, improving mechanization and asset allotment.

6.3. Quantum Figuring

Quantum figuring might present additional opportunities and difficulties for both Half and half and Multi-Cloud procedures, particularly in the domain of cryptography and information handling.

6.4. Green Distributed computing

Manageability concerns will drive associations to take on greener cloud innovations and practices to lessen their carbon impression.

5.1 Embracing Hybrid and Multi-Cloud Environments

In the powerful universe of data innovation, distributed computing has arisen as a groundbreaking power, empowering organizations to improve, scale, and streamline tasks more than ever.

Two noticeable standards inside cloud reception that have gotten some decent forward movement lately are Half breed Cloud and Multi-Cloud conditions. These methodologies offer particular benefits and difficulties, and associations that embrace them decisively are better situated to flourish in the consistently advancing computerized scene.

1. Grasping Half and half Cloud and Multi-Cloud Conditions

1.1. Cross breed Cloud: The Smartest possible scenario

A Cross breed Cloud is a distributed computing model that consolidates components of on-premises foundation or confidential mists with at least one public cloud suppliers. This approach tries to work out some kind of harmony between the control and security of a confidential cloud and the versatility and adaptability of public cloud assets.

In a Cross breed Cloud climate, associations can run crucial applications and store delicate information on their confidential foundation, while using the public cloud to deal with variable jobs, barges popular, or to get to explicit administrations and assets. This crossover approach engages organizations to upgrade their asset portion, decrease costs, and guarantee high accessibility.

1.2. Multi-Cloud: A Different Biological system

Multi-Cloud, then again, is a methodology that includes utilizing different cloud specialist co-ops to meet an association's particular requirements. Dissimilar to Half breed Cloud, Multi-Cloud doesn't be guaranteed to include on-premises foundation; all things considered, it centers around utilizing different public cloud stages at the same time.

The Multi-Cloud technique offers organizations the opportunity to choose the best administrations and estimating models from different suppliers, staying away from seller secure and advancing sound contest among cloud suppliers. It is a proactive way to deal with guarantee high accessibility, calamity recuperation, and business coherence, as assets are dispersed across various cloud conditions.

2. **The Advantages of Embracing Cross breed Cloud and Multi-Cloud Conditions**

2.1. Upgraded Adaptability and Versatility

Embracing Cross breed and Multi-Cloud conditions furnishes associations with unrivaled adaptability and versatility. In Cross breed Cloud arrangements, organizations can flawlessly increase their foundation or down to satisfy fluctuating needs while keeping up with command over basic information. Multi-Cloud conditions offer comparative benefits, empowering asset distribution and scaling as per explicit use cases or geographic areas.

2.2. Cost Streamlining

Cross breed and Multi-Cloud methodologies offer tremendous expense enhancement potential. In a Crossover Cloud, associations can designate assets decisively, keeping away from overprovisioning while at the same time profiting from the expense viability of public mists. Multi-Cloud conditions permit organizations to choose the most financially savvy administrations from different suppliers, upgrading their cloud spending.

2.3. High Accessibility and Strength

Embracing these cloud systems improves high accessibility and strength. In Half breed Mists, associations can plan catastrophe recuperation arrangements that range both private and public mists, guaranteeing business coherence if there should arise an occurrence of unforeseen occasions. Multi-Cloud structures circulate jobs across various suppliers, decreasing the gamble of administration disturbances because of blackouts or different issues.

2.4. Geographic Reach and Information Confinement

Multi-Cloud conditions engage organizations to send assets in server farms situated in various locales or nations, further developing dormancy and giving better client encounters to worldwide clients. This is especially significant for associations with a worldwide presence or those subject to information sway guidelines.

3. **Difficulties and Contemplations**

3.1. Intricacy and Mix

While the advantages of Mixture and Multi-Cloud conditions are significant, overseeing assets across various stages can be complicated. Associations need strong administration and coordination answers for guarantee consistent joining and compelling asset portion.

3.2. Expertise Necessities

Embracing Cross breed and Multi-Cloud conditions requests a different arrangement of abilities and mastery. IT groups should have the information to really oversee different cloud stages and administrations. Consistent preparation and upskilling are fundamental.

3.3. Security and Consistence

Guaranteeing steady security and consistence across various cloud suppliers can challenge. Every supplier might have its own security strategies and controls, requiring cautious preparation and observing to keep a safe climate.

3.4. Cost Administration

Without appropriate expense observing and administration, Half and half and Multi-Cloud conditions can prompt unforeseen expense accelerations and asset spread. Associations should carry out cost administration practices to keep up with effectiveness and control.

4. Carrying out a Cross breed and Multi-Cloud Methodology

4.1. Appraisal and Arranging

The fruitful execution of Mixture and Multi-Cloud methodologies starts with an exhaustive evaluation of an association's ongoing IT scene.

This incorporates an assessment of utilizations, information, jobs, and business targets. An unmistakable movement and organization plan ought to be created in view of these evaluations.

4.2. Framework as Code (IaC)

Embracing Foundation as Code (IaC) practices can essentially work on the provisioning and the board of assets in Half and half and Multi-Cloud conditions. IaC empowers associations to robotize the creation and setup of foundation, guaranteeing consistency and lessening manual blunders.

4.3. Cloud The executives and Organization

Putting resources into cloud the board and organization devices is fundamental for compelling asset administration across Crossover and Multi-Cloud conditions. These instruments give perceivability, mechanization, and incorporated control, making it simpler to oversee complex structures.

4.4. Security and Consistence

Carrying out a vigorous security methodology is central. Character and access the executives, encryption, and consistence controls should be customized to the particular prerequisites of Half and half and Multi-Cloud conditions. Consistent checking and evaluating are basic for keeping up with security.

In the present computerized period, embracing Half breed and Multi-Cloud conditions is at this point not a decision yet an essential basic for organizations planning to remain cutthroat and deft. These cloud methodologies offer a fair methodology that joins control, versatility, cost-productivity, and strength.

While they accompany difficulties connected with intricacy, expertise necessities, security, and cost administration, these difficulties can be overwhelmed with cautious preparation, the right instruments, and a promise to progressing learning and improvement. At last, associations that embrace Cross breed and Multi-Cloud conditions decisively will wind up better prepared to adjust to developing business needs and flourish in the consistently changing mechanical scene.

5.2 Advantages and Challenges of Hybrid Cloud

In the domain of distributed computing, organizations are progressively going to crossover cloud answers for tackle the most ideal scenario - the security and control of on-premises foundation and the adaptability and versatility of public cloud administrations. This approach offers a special arrangement of benefits and difficulties that associations should cautiously consider while embracing cross breed cloud techniques.

Benefits of Half and half Cloud

1. **Adaptability and Adaptability**

   One of the essential benefits of half and half cloud is its versatility and adaptability. Associations can powerfully dispense assets between on-premises foundation and public cloud administrations depending on the situation. During times of popularity, they can take advantage of the tremendous processing force of the public cloud, and when responsibilities decline, they can downsize to save costs. This flexibility permits organizations to streamline asset use without over-provisioning.

2. **Cost Effectiveness**

   Mixture cloud offers cost-proficiency by permitting associations to coordinate their responsibilities with the most practical framework. On-premises assets can be utilized for consistent, unsurprising jobs, while the public cloud can deal with variable or bursty responsibilities. This approach guarantees that organizations pay just for the assets they use, decreasing capital consumptions.

3. **Information Control and Security**

   Crossover cloud empowers associations to keep up with command over their basic information and applications. Delicate data can be put away on-premises servers or confidential cloud conditions, guaranteeing consistence with administrative prerequisites and information security norms. Public cloud administrations can be utilized for less touchy responsibilities, exploiting the cloud supplier's hearty security highlights.

4. **Fiasco Recuperation and Business Congruity**

   Half breed cloud designs work with powerful calamity recuperation and business coherence arrangements. By imitating information and applications across both on-premises and public cloud conditions, associations can guarantee the accessibility of their frameworks even in case of a disastrous disappointment. This overt repetitiveness improves strength and limits free time.

5. **Geographic Reach and Low Inactivity**

   Half and half cloud empowers organizations to send assets in server farms situated in various geographic locales. This dispersion further develops inactivity, guaranteeing quick and responsive administrations for clients all over the planet. It's especially significant for associations serving worldwide business sectors.

6. **Inheritance Framework Combination**

Many undertakings have put vigorously in heritage frameworks that won't be quickly moved to the cloud. Crossover cloud permits these associations to incorporate their current framework with cloud administrations, utilizing their inheritance speculations while slowly modernizing their IT climate.

Difficulties of Cross breed Cloud

1. **Intricacy**

   The intricacy of overseeing assets across various conditions is one of the essential difficulties of cross breed cloud. Associations should manage divergent advances, structures, and the board apparatuses. This intricacy can prompt coordination troubles and increment the expectation to learn and adapt for IT groups.

2. **Information Mix**

   Incorporating information between on-premises and cloud conditions can be testing, particularly while managing various information configurations, designs, and conventions. Guaranteeing that information streams consistently between these conditions is critical for keeping up with productive activities.

3. **Security Concerns**

   While cross breed cloud offers improved security through information isolation, it additionally presents new security concerns. Overseeing access controls, encryption, and validation across both on-premises and cloud conditions requires fastidious preparation and execution. Any misconfiguration or oversight can prompt security weaknesses.

4. **Merchant Lock-In**

   Reliance on a particular cloud supplier's administrations or innovations can prompt seller secure in, restricting an association's capacity to switch suppliers or adjust to changing business needs. Moderating merchant secure is a basic thought while taking on a half breed cloud procedure.

5. **Cost Administration**

   Without viable expense the board rehearses, associations might encounter startling expense accelerations. Observing and improving costs across both on-premises and cloud conditions are fundamental to abstain from overspending and asset spread.

6. **Expertise Necessities**

   Dealing with a half breed cloud climate requires a different range of abilities. IT groups should be capable in both on-premises foundation and cloud advancements. Nonstop preparation and expertise improvement are fundamental to guarantee that the association can successfully explore the intricacies of a mixture cloud climate.

7. **Administration and Consistence**

Keeping up with administration and consistence across mixture conditions can challenge. Associations need to lay out predictable arrangements and controls for information, security, and consistence, while additionally guaranteeing that these approaches are implemented consistently across all framework parts.

Crossover cloud arrangements offer associations a convincing blend of versatility, cost-proficiency, information control, and adaptability. In any case, they accompany their reasonable portion of difficulties that require cautious thought and proactive administration.

To effectively use the upsides of mixture cloud while relieving its difficulties, associations ought to put resources into powerful administration and arrangement instruments, focus on security and consistence, execute cost enhancement rehearses, and give continuous preparation and ability advancement for their IT groups. With the right system and approach, organizations can bridle the force of cross breed cloud to meet their developing IT needs and drive advanced change in the present speedy business scene.

5.3 Managing Complexity and Ensuring Consistency

In the present quickly advancing computerized scene, organizations are depending on progressively complex IT foundations to remain serious and satisfy client needs. While these perplexing conditions offer a scope of advantages, they likewise bring huge difficulties connected with overseeing intricacy and guaranteeing consistency. This article investigates the significance of these angles and gives bits of knowledge into powerful techniques to address them.

The Developing Intricacy of IT Conditions

Multicloud Reception: Numerous associations presently influence different cloud suppliers and administrations to meet their assorted registering needs. This multicloud approach offers adaptability however presents intricacy regarding incorporation, the executives, and administration.

Half and half Framework: Cross breed conditions, consolidating on-premises server farms with cloud assets, have become normal. This blend of physical and virtual resources adds intricacy to framework the executives.

Different Innovations: Organizations progressively depend on a great many advancements, from containerization and microservices to edge figuring and Web of Things (IoT) gadgets. Every one of these innovations brings its own arrangement of intricacies.

Administrative Consistence: As information security and administrative necessities become more severe, guaranteeing consistence across complex IT conditions turns into a need. This incorporates overseeing information access, encryption, and review trails.

The Significance of Overseeing Intricacy

Functional Proficiency: Intricacy can prompt failures, expanding functional expenses and ruining dexterity. Improving on complex cycles and framework can bring about additional effective activities.

Dependability and Versatility: Intricacy can present weak spots and increment the gamble of framework blackouts. Streamlining and normalizing basic parts can further develop unwavering quality and flexibility.

Security: Intricacy frequently prompts security weaknesses, as it becomes testing to screen and deal with each part of the climate. A rearranged and efficient framework is more straightforward to get.

Adaptability: Improved and very much oversaw frameworks are simpler to scale as business needs advance. Intricacy can block versatility endeavors.

Procedures for Overseeing Intricacy and Guaranteeing Consistency

Normalization: Normalizing innovations, cycles, and setups is an essential move toward overseeing intricacy. Associations ought to characterize and uphold guidelines for equipment, programming, and techniques to establish consistency across the climate.

Mechanization: Robotization apparatuses and contents can assist with smoothing out dull errands, diminishing the gamble of human mistake and accelerating processes. Computerization can be applied to provisioning, design the executives, and observing assignments.

Framework as Code (IaC): Embracing IaC permits associations to characterize and oversee foundation utilizing code. This approach guarantees that foundation setups are steady, rendition controlled, and effectively reproducible.

Design The board: Carry out strong arrangement the executives practices to guarantee that frameworks are reliably designed by predefined principles. Devices like Ansible, Manikin, and Gourmet expert can aid this cycle.

DevOps and Ceaseless Combination/Nonstop Sending (CI/Cd): Taking on DevOps practices and CI/Album pipelines can smooth out programming advancement and arrangement processes, guaranteeing that applications and administrations are reliably fabricated, tried, and sent.

Cloud The executives and Arrangement: In multicloud and half and half conditions, cloud the board and organization stages give perceivability and control. They assist associations with overseeing assets productively and reliably across cloud suppliers.

Observing and Investigation: Carry out exhaustive checking and examination answers for gain perceivability into the exhibition, security, and consistence of IT conditions. Constant experiences can help recognize and resolve issues expeditiously.

Containerization and Microservices: Containerization advances like Docker and compartment coordination stages like Kubernetes work on application arrangement and the board. Microservices models advance seclusion and simplicity of support.

Security Arrangements and Access Controls: Characterize and uphold security strategies reliably across all layers of the IT climate. Execute powerful access controls and verification components to guarantee information security.

Documentation and Information Sharing: Keep up with exceptional documentation of designs, cycles, and best practices. Empower information dividing between IT groups to guarantee that everybody is lined up with principles and techniques.

Challenges in Overseeing Intricacy

Expertise Hole: Overseeing complex IT conditions requires a gifted labor force. Associations might confront difficulties in recruiting and holding ability with the essential skill.

Costs: Executing robotization, normalization, and checking arrangements can require critical forthright venture. Be that as it may, the drawn out benefits frequently offset these expenses.

Protection from Change: Representatives might oppose changes to laid out cycles and work processes. Compelling change the board techniques are fundamental to conquer opposition.

Heritage Frameworks: Numerous associations have inheritance frameworks that are intrinsically complicated and testing to coordinate with present day IT rehearses. Inheritance framework modernization endeavors can be tedious and expensive.

Versatility: As organizations develop, their IT surroundings become more perplexing. Overseeing intricacy at scale can especially challenge.

In the present unique IT scene, overseeing intricacy and guaranteeing consistency are critical for accomplishing functional effectiveness, keeping up with security, and driving development. Associations should embrace procedures like normalization, mechanization, IaC, and DevOps to work on complex conditions.

While overseeing intricacy isn't without its difficulties, the advantages of a rearranged and steady IT climate, including further developed effectiveness, unwavering quality, and security, put forth the attempt beneficial. By focusing on these procedures and encouraging a culture of nonstop improvement, organizations can explore the intricacies of the cutting edge IT scene no sweat and certainty.

Chapter 6

Cloud-Native Technologies and Innovations

The universe of innovation is in a steady condition of transition, and as organizations and associations endeavor to stay cutthroat in the computerized age, they should adjust to new standards and approaches. Quite possibly of the most groundbreaking change as of late has been the rise of cloud-local advancements and the related developments that have reformed how applications are created, sent, and made due. In this exhaustive investigation, we will dig profound into the domain of cloud-local advancements and developments, grasping their advancement, center standards, and the effect they have had on different ventures. From containerization and microservices to serverless processing and coordination, we will look at the structure blocks of the cloud-local biological system and how they have reshaped the computerized scene.

The Advancement of Cloud-Local Innovations

To comprehend cloud-local innovations, we should initially follow their developmental excursion. Customary solid applications, portrayed by their enormous and firmly coupled codebases, were once the standard. These applications presented difficulties concerning adaptability, practicality, and arrangement. Notwithstanding, the appearance of virtualization and the broad reception of distributed computing denoted a critical defining moment.

Virtualization considered the deliberation of actual equipment, empowering various virtual machines (VMs) to run on a solitary actual server. This innovation improved asset use however didn't essentially have an impact on how applications were architected or sent. Distributed computing stages, for example, Amazon Web Administrations (AWS), Microsoft Purplish blue, and Google Cloud Stage (GCP), further sped up the shift by offering versatile, on-request framework administrations.

Compartments and Holder Coordination

Compartments arose as a distinct advantage in the cloud-local scene. Docker, specifically, assumed a critical part in promoting compartment innovation. Holders bundle applications and their conditions into separated units, giving consistency across various conditions. This approach empowers engineers to make, test, and convey applications all the more proficiently.

Compartment arrangement stages, like Kubernetes, became a force to be reckoned with to deal with the organization, scaling, and coordination of holders at scale.

Kubernetes, initially created by Google, has turned into the true norm for compartment coordination, empowering associations to robotize complex sending work processes and accomplish elevated degrees of strength and adaptability.

Microservices Design

Microservices engineering is one more basic part of cloud-local turn of events. Dissimilar to solid applications, microservices separate applications into little, approximately coupled administrations that can be created, sent, and scaled freely. This approach advances readiness, permitting groups to repeat on individual administrations without influencing the whole application.

Microservices cultivate a culture of consistent joining and persistent conveyance (CI/Cd), where changes can be quickly tried and sent. This approach lines up with the standards of DevOps, underlining cooperation among advancement and activities groups to accomplish quicker, more dependable programming conveyance.

Serverless Processing

Serverless processing takes the idea of cloud-local to a higher level. In serverless designs, engineers center exclusively around composing code, without worrying about server provisioning or the board. Cloud suppliers, like AWS Lambda, Purplish blue Capabilities, and Google Cloud Capabilities, handle the hidden foundation.

Serverless registering is occasion driven, with capabilities executing because of occasions, for example, HTTP demands, data set updates, or record transfers. This approach offers auto-scaling, cost effectiveness, and diminished functional above, making it especially engaging for specific use cases, for example, web APIs and occasion driven applications.

Cloud-Local Developments

Istio and Administration Lattices: Istio is an open-source administration network that gives progressed traffic the executives, security, and recognizability for microservices. Administration networks like Istio assist associations with dealing with the intricacy of microservices correspondence and guarantee dependability.

Prometheus and Grafana: These checking and discernibleness instruments have acquired fame for their capacity to gather and imagine measurements from containerized applications and microservices. They assume a vital part in figuring out framework execution and distinguishing issues progressively.

Steerage and Bundle The board: Rudder works on the organization of uses on Kubernetes by characterizing, introducing, and updating even complex applications as Kubernetes outlines. It smoothes out the bundling and appropriation of cloud-local applications.

GitOps: GitOps is a functional model that use Git stores as the single wellspring of truth for framework and application designs. This approach advances straightforwardness, forming, and computerization in overseeing cloud-local conditions.

CNCF Tasks: The Cloud Local Processing Establishment (CNCF) has a great many undertakings and devices, including Prometheus, Rudder, and Kubernetes itself. These ventures are at the front line of cloud-local development and act as an asset for associations hoping to take on cloud-local innovations.

Influence on Enterprises

Monetary Administrations: Monetary foundations influence cloud-local advances to upgrade their computerized contributions, further develop security, and smooth out consistence. Cloud-local arrangements empower constant information handling, misrepresentation identification, and customized client encounters.

Medical services: Medical care associations saddle cloud-local advances to safely store and break down immense measures of patient information. Telemedicine stages, wellbeing checking gadgets, and information driven research benefit from the adaptability and nimbleness presented by cloud-local methodologies.

Internet business: Internet business stages depend on microservices and containerization to deal with fluctuating traffic loads, guarantee high accessibility, and give consistent client encounters. Serverless capabilities are utilized for errands like picture resizing and request handling.

Gaming: The gaming business use cloud-local advances for multiplayer gaming, content conveyance, and constant investigation. Versatile backends, containerized game servers, and serverless capabilities improve gaming encounters and lessen framework costs.

Auto: Associated vehicles and independent driving frameworks depend on cloud-local designs to handle information from sensors, speak with different vehicles, and get over-the-air refreshes. This innovation speeds up development in the car area.

Fabricating: Cloud-local arrangements support prescient upkeep, production network improvement, and cycle computerization in assembling. IoT gadgets and edge registering joined with cloud-local backends empower ongoing bits of knowledge and proficiency upgrades.

Difficulties and Contemplations

Intricacy: Overseeing microservices, holders, and serverless capabilities can be intricate. Associations need talented groups and the right instruments to really explore this intricacy.

Security: Security in a cloud-local climate requires an extensive system, including secure compartment pictures, access controls, and danger recognition. Misconfigurations and weaknesses can prompt information breaks.

Cost Administration: While cloud-local advancements can give cost reserve funds through asset improvement, they can likewise prompt startling costs on the off chance that not oversaw cautiously. Associations should screen utilization and take on savvy rehearses.

Social Shift: Embracing cloud-local practices frequently requires a social shift inside associations. Groups need to embrace coordinated effort, mechanization, and a mentality of consistent improvement.

Cloud-local advancements and developments have changed the computerized scene, empowering associations to fabricate, send, and scale applications with remarkable speed and effectiveness. From containerization and microservices to serverless figuring and coordination, these advancements have introduced another time of spryness and strength in programming improvement.

As the cloud-local biological system keeps on advancing, associations across different businesses will have the valuable chance to open additional opportunities, improve quicker, and convey upgraded encounters to their clients. Notwithstanding, outcome in the cloud-local excursion requires a mix of specialized mastery, a culture of cooperation, and a guarantee to consistent learning and improvement.

In this powerful and steadily advancing scene, remaining informed about the most recent turns of events and best practices is pivotal for associations hoping to outfit the maximum capacity of cloud-local advancements. As we push ahead, the cloud-local upheaval makes it clear that things are not pulling back, and its effect on the advanced world will undoubtedly be considerably more significant in the years to come.

6.1 The Role of Cloud-Native Technologies (Containers, Serverless, Microservices)

Cloud-local innovations have become fundamental to current programming advancement and IT activities. In a time where readiness, versatility, and effectiveness are foremost, these advancements — compartments, serverless processing, and microservices — assume a vital part in empowering associations to flourish in the computerized age. In this investigation, we will dig into the jobs and meaning of these cloud-local advancements and how they have reshaped the scene of programming improvement and arrangement.

Holders: Seclusion and Movability

Holders have reformed how applications are bundled and sent. They give a lightweight and steady climate that embodies an application and its conditions, guaranteeing that it runs dependably across various processing conditions.

One of the critical jobs of compartments is detachment. Every compartment runs freely, disengaged from different holders on a similar host. This confinement improves security and steadiness by forestalling clashes among applications and their conditions.

Designers can unhesitatingly assemble and test applications in a single climate and afterward send them in another, realizing that the compartment will act reliably.

Compartments likewise work with conveyability. They conceptual the basic framework, permitting applications to run consistently on any stage that upholds the compartment runtime, like Docker or containerd. This versatility works on the method involved with moving applications between on-premises server farms and public mists or even between various cloud suppliers. It decreases seller secure and engages associations with more noteworthy adaptability in picking their arrangement targets.

Holders are especially appropriate for microservices structures. Every microservice can be bundled in a different holder, empowering free turn of events, scaling, and organization. Holder arrangement stages like

Kubernetes give devices to overseeing compartments at scale, robotizing errands, for example, load adjusting, scaling, and self-mending, making holders a fundamental structure block for current cloud-local applications.

Serverless Figuring: Occasion Driven Versatility

Serverless figuring addresses a change in perspective in cloud-local advances. It abstracts away the administration of server foundation, permitting engineers to zero in exclusively on composing code to execute capabilities in light of occasions.

At the center of serverless registering is occasion driven adaptability. Capabilities are conjured in light of occasions, for example, HTTP demands, data set changes, or record transfers. The cloud supplier naturally scales the framework to deal with the responsibility, and engineers are charged in light of the genuine asset utilization, frequently in millisecond increases.

Serverless figuring is especially appropriate for situations with inconsistent or capricious jobs. It disposes of the need to arrangement and oversee servers, which can be exorbitant and complex. All things considered, designers characterize works and depend on the cloud supplier to deal with the fundamental foundation.

One of the critical jobs of serverless registering is cost effectiveness. Associations pay just for the register assets utilized during capability execution, which can bring about massive expense investment funds contrasted with customary server-based approaches. Furthermore, serverless models advance fast turn of events and arrangement, as engineers can zero in on coding rather than foundation provisioning.

Serverless additionally works on the most common way of building versatile and shortcoming open minded applications. Cloud suppliers handle the scaling and dispersion of capability execution, guaranteeing that applications can deal with traffic spikes and disappointments smoothly. This empowers designers to construct exceptionally accessible and strong frameworks with less exertion.

Microservices: Readiness and Adaptability

Microservices engineering is a product configuration approach where applications are made out of little, freely deployable administrations that impart through APIs. This design style has acquired gigantic fame because of its capacity to improve nimbleness and versatility.

One of the essential jobs of microservices is dexterity. By separating applications into more modest administrations, improvement groups can deal with individual parts freely. This decoupling of administrations considers quicker improvement cycles, as changes to one microservice don't need broad relapse testing of the whole application.

Microservices additionally empower adaptability. Each assistance can be scaled autonomously in light of its particular asset prerequisites and request. This fine-grained versatility guarantees that assets are assigned where they are required most, upgrading cost effectiveness and execution.

One more benefit of microservices is shortcoming separation. At the point when one assistance experiences an issue or fizzles, it doesn't be guaranteed to influence the whole application. Administrations can be planned with overt repetitiveness and failover components to keep up with generally speaking framework accessibility even notwithstanding part disappointments.

Be that as it may, dealing with a microservices engineering presents its own arrangement of difficulties. Associations should put resources into strong assistance revelation, load adjusting, and arrangement components to guarantee that administrations can convey really and are versatile to disappointments. Also, checking and discernibleness are basic to figuring out the way of behaving of disseminated frameworks.

Consolidating Cloud-Local Advancements

While compartments, serverless figuring, and microservices each play their one of a kind parts and benefits, they are not totally unrelated. As a matter of fact, associations frequently join these innovations to saddle their reciprocal assets.

For instance, a microservices engineering can be containerized, permitting every microservice to run in its own holder. Holder organization stages like Kubernetes can deal with the sending and scaling of these compartments. This mix offers the advantages of both microservices and containerization: dexterity, adaptability, and detachment.

Serverless capabilities can likewise be coordinated into microservices designs. For undertakings that require fast and occasion driven execution, serverless capabilities can be utilized close by microservices. This half and half methodology permits associations to improve asset usage and cost while keeping up with the advantages of microservices and serverless processing.

Besides, associations can utilize serverless figuring to improve the occasion driven capacities of their microservices. Serverless capabilities can be set off by occasions from microservices, giving an exceptionally responsive and versatile environment.

All in all, cloud-local advancements have changed how applications are created, sent, and made due. Compartments give disconnection and convenientce, empowering steady application conduct across different conditions. Serverless registering offers occasion driven versatility and cost proficiency, abstracting away server the executives. Microservices engineering improves dexterity and adaptability, empowering fast turn of events and free scaling.

While every one of these cloud-local advancements fills explicit needs, they are not fundamentally unrelated and can be consolidated to make strong and adaptable application structures. As associations proceed to take on and adjust these advancements, they will be better prepared to fulfill the needs of the computerized age, conveying creative arrangements with nimbleness and productivity. The jobs of compartments, serverless processing, and microservices will keep on advancing as innovation propels and new use cases arise, forming the fate of cloud-local turn of events.

6.2 Leveraging AI and ML in Cloud Environments

Man-made brainpower (artificial intelligence) and AI (ML) are driving development across ventures, reshaping the manner in which organizations work, and conveying improved encounters to clients. When joined with the capacities of distributed computing, these innovations arrive at new levels of adaptability, proficiency, and openness. In this investigation, we will dive into how artificial intelligence and ML are utilized in cloud conditions, the extraordinary effect they have, and the difficulties and open doors they present.

1. **Versatility and Flexibility**

   One of the main benefits of conveying computer based intelligence and ML in cloud conditions is versatility. Conventional on-premises framework frequently misses the mark on adaptability to deal with the computational requests of artificial intelligence and ML responsibilities, which can be profoundly asset escalated. Cloud suppliers, for example, Amazon Web Administrations (AWS), Microsoft Purplish blue, and Google Cloud Stage (GCP), offer the capacity to increase processing assets or down on-request.

   For example, while preparing a profound learning model, requiring significant computational power is normal. Cloud stages permit associations to arrangement strong GPU occasions for preparing and afterward downsize when not being used. This flexibility guarantees that assets are assigned effectively, decreasing functional expenses and time-to-knowledge.

2. **Information Openness and Capacity**

   Computer based intelligence and ML depend vigorously on information. Cloud conditions give brought together, versatile information stockpiling arrangements that work with information access, the executives, and investigation.

   Cloud-based information distribution centers, information lakes, and item stockpiling administrations empower associations to store tremendous measures of organized and unstructured information safely and cost-successfully.

   Furthermore, cloud suppliers offer various information examination and handling administrations that can be flawlessly incorporated with artificial intelligence and ML work processes. This collaboration permits information researchers and specialists to get to and preprocess information proficiently, an essential move toward the AI pipeline.

3. **Artificial intelligence Administrations and APIs**

Cloud suppliers offer a rich environment of man-made intelligence administrations and APIs that theoretical away the intricacies of building and preparing AI models without any preparation. These administrations cover an extensive variety of simulated intelligence capacities, including regular language handling (NLP), PC vision, discourse acknowledgment, and that's only the tip of the iceberg.

For instance, AWS gives Amazon Rekognition to picture and video examination, Amazon Understand for NLP assignments, and Amazon Polly for text-to-discourse blend. Also, Sky blue offers Sky blue Mental Administrations, including Vision man-made intelligence, Language man-made intelligence, and Discourse simulated intelligence.

These pre-assembled computer based intelligence administrations are open through APIs, making it clear for engineers to integrate simulated intelligence usefulness into their applications. This openness speeds up the improvement interaction and brings the obstruction down to section for associations hoping to bridle man-made intelligence abilities.

4. **AI Structures and Devices**

Cloud conditions are outfitted with a variety of AI systems and apparatuses that improve on model turn of events and arrangement. TensorFlow, PyTorch, scikit-learn, and MXNet are only a couple of instances of well known ML systems accessible in the cloud.

Additionally, cloud stages give oversaw ML benefits that deal mechanized AI (AutoML) abilities. These administrations smooth out the model preparation process, consequently choosing calculations, hyperparameters, and preprocessing methods, permitting associations to fabricate ML models with negligible manual mediation.

5. **Appropriated Registering and Equal Handling**

   Artificial intelligence and ML jobs frequently benefit from disseminated registering and equal handling, where assignments are split between different figure assets to facilitate handling. Cloud conditions are appropriate for such undertakings, as they give conveyed registering administrations and devices that empower parallelism.

   For instance, AWS offers administrations like SageMaker for circulated model preparation and Flexible MapReduce (EMR) for large information handling.

   GCP gives Google Cloud ML Motor and Dataflow for comparable purposes. These administrations dynamic the intricacies of setting up and overseeing disseminated foundation, permitting associations to zero in on model turn of events and information examination.

6. **Man-made intelligence Driven Robotization**

Man-made intelligence controlled robotization is changing different parts of cloud activities and the board. Cloud suppliers are coordinating simulated intelligence and ML into their administrations to upgrade security, decrease costs, and advance asset designation.

One remarkable application is the utilization of artificial intelligence driven peculiarity recognition to screen cloud framework and recognize surprising conduct demonstrative of safety dangers or asset shortcomings. These frameworks can naturally set off reactions, like scaling assets, secluding compromised cases, or producing cautions.

Difficulties and Contemplations

Cost Administration: Cloud assets can become costly on the off chance that not oversaw really. Associations should screen asset use intently, use cost investigation instruments, and carry out cost-saving measures to stay away from startling consumptions.

Information Protection and Security: Taking care of delicate information in the cloud requires powerful safety efforts. Encryption, access controls, and consistence with information insurance guidelines are basic to guaranteeing information protection and security.

Information Administration: Legitimate information administration rehearses are fundamental to keep up with information quality, consistency, and consistence. Associations should lay out information administration arrangements and methods to really oversee information.

Ability and Abilities: Building and sending artificial intelligence and ML arrangements in the cloud requires particular abilities. Associations might have to put resources into preparing or recruit talented experts to explore this mind boggling scene.

Moral Contemplations: The utilization of simulated intelligence and ML brings up moral issues around inclination, decency, and straightforwardness. Associations should be cautious in tending to these worries and guaranteeing capable simulated intelligence rehearses.

The mix of man-made intelligence and ML with cloud conditions addresses a considerable combination of innovations that is changing enterprises and reforming business tasks. The adaptability, availability of information, pre-constructed simulated intelligence administrations, AI systems, dispersed processing capacities, and robotization elements of cloud stages are moving associations towards imaginative arrangements and improved independent direction.

Notwithstanding, associations should move toward this joining with an unmistakable system that tends to cost administration, information protection and security, administration, ability obtaining, and moral contemplations.

As computer based intelligence and ML proceed to progress and cloud suppliers refine their contributions, the cooperative energy between these innovations and cloud conditions will just turn out to be all the more remarkable, reshaping ventures and pushing associations into an information driven, wise future.

6.3 Edge Computing and Its Impact on Cloud

In the always advancing scene of innovation, two ideas have acquired huge unmistakable quality as of late: Edge Figuring and Distributed computing. These two ideal models have not just changed the manner in which we ponder registering yet additionally significantly affect one another. In this article, we will dig into the universe of Edge Processing and investigate its harmonious relationship with Distributed computing, revealing insight into the ramifications for ventures, organizations, and the eventual fate of figuring itself.

Understanding Edge Registering

Edge Processing is a circulated figuring worldview that carries calculation and information stockpiling nearer to the wellspring of information age or utilization. Not at all like conventional Distributed computing, which concentrates information handling in server farms, Edge Registering pushes handling power and information stockpiling out to the "edge" of the organization, closer to where information is made and required. This shift has become fundamental because of the developing interest for ongoing information handling, diminished dormancy, and expanded protection and security.

The Critical Parts of Edge Processing

Edge Gadgets: These are the equipment and sensors conveyed at the edge of the organization, like IoT gadgets, cell phones, independent vehicles, and modern machines. They create huge measures of information and frequently require moment reaction times.

Edge Servers: These are limited scale server farms situated at the edge of the organization, nearer to the edge gadgets. They have applications and administrations expected for handling and dissecting information locally.

Edge Cloud: This is a decentralized foundation that consolidates Edge Servers and Distributed computing assets. It empowers the consistent organization and the executives of figuring assets across the edge and the cloud.

Benefits of Edge Processing

Low Dormancy: Edge Registering fundamentally diminishes the time it takes for information to venture out from the source to the handling unit. This is basic for applications like independent vehicles, where even milliseconds of deferral can have dangerous results.

Transmission capacity Effectiveness: By handling information locally, Edge Figuring diminishes the need to send huge volumes of information to concentrated server farms, in this way improving organization transfer speed and bringing down functional expenses.

Improved Protection and Security: Since delicate information can be handled locally, it is less helpless against security penetrates that might happen during information transmission to far off server farms.

Adaptability: Edge Registering takes into consideration the simple versatility of figuring assets as more edge gadgets are conveyed, guaranteeing that the framework can deal with expanding jobs effectively.

Influence on Distributed computing

Integral Relationship: Edge Figuring and Distributed computing are not contenders but instead correlative advancements. They cooperate to make a half and half biological system that outfits the qualities of the two standards. The cloud gives capacity, complex information investigation, and administrations that are unreasonable to send at the edge, while Edge Figuring handles ongoing information handling and low-inactivity applications.

Half and half Cloud Models: Associations are progressively embracing crossover cloud designs that coordinate Edge Registering assets with public and confidential mists. This approach offers the adaptability to pick the best area for explicit responsibilities in light of dormancy, security, and consistence prerequisites.

Decreased Cloud Information Move: Edge Registering lessens how much information that should be moved to the cloud. This recoveries transfer speed costs as well as limits the gamble of information bottlenecks and guarantees effective information the executives.

Edge-Cloud Collaboration: The cooperative energy between Edge Processing and Distributed computing empowers additional opportunities for applications like increased reality, augmented reality, and continuous examination. Information can be handled at the edge for sure fire client communication while additionally being shipped off the cloud for more profound investigation and capacity.

Challenges for Cloud Suppliers: Cloud specialist organizations are adjusting to the Edge Registering pattern by offering administrations like AWS Greengrass and Purplish blue IoT Edge. These administrations stretch out cloud capacities to the edge and empower consistent mix with existing cloud foundation.

Influence on Ventures and Organizations

Producing: Makers can utilize Edge Registering to upgrade mechanization and prescient support. Machines at the plant floor can handle information locally to recognize and resolve issues progressively, diminishing margin time and upkeep costs.

Medical services: In medical services, Edge Registering empowers distant patient checking, ongoing information examination in clinical gadgets, and speedier reaction times in basic circumstances, at last working on tolerant consideration.

Retail: Retailers can use Edge Processing for stock administration, in-store client examination, and customized showcasing, offering a consistent shopping experience.

Transportation: Edge Registering assumes a urgent part in independent vehicles, empowering them to go with split-subsequent options in view of nearby sensor information. This is crucial for guaranteeing security and productivity on the streets.

Brilliant Urban areas: Edge Registering adds to the improvement of savvy urban communities by supporting applications like traffic the board, squander the executives, and ecological observing.

Media communications: Telecom organizations benefit from Edge Processing by decreasing the heap on their organizations and working on the nature of administrations. Edge servers can reserve and convey content nearer to end-clients, lessening idleness in mixed media web based and web administrations.

The Eventual fate of Processing

As we look forward, obviously Edge Processing isn't simply a pattern yet a basic change by they way we approach figuring. It permits us to saddle the maximum capacity of the Web of Things (IoT), 5G organizations, and arising innovations like man-made intelligence and AI.

The harmonious connection between Edge Processing and Distributed computing makes ready for a more flexible and responsive registering environment. It empowers us to adjust the requests of constant information handling with the scale and adaptability of the cloud. This blend is vital for accomplishing the objectives of Industry 4.0, independent frameworks, and the computerized change of enterprises.

Chapter 7

Skill Development and Workforce Transformation

Skill development and workforce transformation have become critical aspects for individuals, organizations, and nations in today's quickly changing labor market. The nature of employment is changing due to ongoing technological improvements, globalization, and demographic changes. As a result, people must constantly learn new skills to remain competitive in the job market. Furthermore, governments and businesses everywhere are realizing that in order to meet the changing needs of the economy, the workforce must be transformed and support for skill development must be given. The significance of skill development and workforce transformation will be discussed in this article, along with methods for addressing the shifting demands of the labor market.

The Significance of Developing Skills

1. **Flexibility in Response to Technological Developments**
   Technological advancements like robotics, automation, and artificial intelligence are upending traditional jobs and opening up new career opportunities. People in the digital age must constantly learn new skills and update their existing ones in order

to remain relevant. For instance, in order to move into positions involving dealing with automated systems, an individual in the manufacturing sector might need to acquire programming or data analytics skills. By developing their skills, people may make sure they have what they need to embrace technology and adapt to the ever-changing nature of the labor market.

2. **Improving One's Employability**

   The market for jobs is competitive, and having the right skills can make a person much more employable. Candidates with a broad range of abilities that meet their company's needs are more in demand by employers. People can set themselves apart from their colleagues and improve their chances of securing attractive employment opportunities by investing in skill development. Additionally, ongoing skill improvement reduces the possibility of becoming outdated due to technology breakthroughs, which guarantees job stability.

3. **Encouraging Professional Development and Contentment**

The improvement of one's skills is essential for promoting professional advancement and job happiness. People can take on more demanding and fulfilling responsibilities and broaden their scope of work by learning new skills. This boosts motivation and job satisfaction in addition to offering chances for professional advancement. Additionally, developing one's skills enables one to consider alternative career routes, which improves one's employability and job chances in general.

Workforce Transformation's Significance

1. **Satisfying the Digital Economy's Needs**

   Prompt innovation, greater connectedness, and improved productivity define the digital economy. Organizations must reshape their workforce by providing workers with the digital skills they need to be competitive. This shift entails promoting a continuous learning culture and assisting in the incorporation of digital technologies into work processes. Organizations may foster innovation, increase operational effectiveness, and successfully compete in the digital age by modernizing their workforce.

2. Filling up the Skill Gaps

The difference between the skills held by the workforce and the skills needed in the labor market is referred to as a "skill gap." The goal of workforce transformation is to close these skill gaps by providing initiatives for upskilling and specialized training. Organizations may guarantee that their workforce has the skills needed to meet the changing needs of the labor market by addressing skill gaps. This helps the company as well as encourages worker engagement and retention.

Techniques for Developing Skills and Transforming the Workforce

1. **Industry and Educational Institutions Working Together**
   Industry and educational institutions working together is essential to making sure that the skills being taught fit the demands of the labor market. Through forming collaborations, academic institutions can acquire valuable understanding of industry demands and modify their course offerings accordingly. Joint research projects, internships, and apprenticeships are some examples of this kind of cooperation. Industry experts may also be invited to speak as guest lecturers and provide their firsthand knowledge. This cooperative strategy guarantees that graduates have the abilities and know-how needed to be successful in the workforce.

2. **Making a Lifelong Learning Investment**
   The constant acquisition and development of abilities throughout a person's career is referred to as lifelong learning. To stay relevant in the face of shifting employment needs, people must make the investment in lifelong learning. By providing funding for skill-development programs, online learning environments,

and incentives for staff to take time off for training and upskilling, governments and organizations may play a critical role in fostering lifelong learning. People and organizations can remain ahead of the curve and adjust to the shifting demands of the labor market by promoting a culture of lifelong learning.

3. **Initiatives for Reskilling and Upskilling**

Initiatives for reskilling and upskilling are crucial for closing skill gaps and promoting workforce change. While reskilling is teaching employees completely new skill sets, upskilling entails improving employees' current skill sets to conform to evolving trends. Companies may put these ideas into action by providing career development pathways, mentorship opportunities, and training courses. Governments can also fund and incentivize upskilling and reskilling programs financially. Organizations may secure long-term success and future-proof their employees by funding these projects.

To prosper in the rapidly changing global economy, people, businesses, and countries must prioritize skill development and workforce transformation. Rapid technological improvements have changed the nature of employment, making it necessary to continuously acquire and improve skills. Through workforce transformation and skill development investments, we can guarantee that people have the skills needed to adjust to a changing labor market. Key solutions to handle the changing demands of the labor market include upskilling and reskilling efforts, investment in lifelong learning, and collaboration between educational institutions and business. We can create a knowledgeable and adaptable workforce that stimulates economic growth, productivity, and creativity by adopting these tactics.

7.1 Addressing the Cloud Skills Gap in India

All throughout the world, cloud computing is becoming more and more popular, and India is no exception. Many advantages, including cost savings, scalability, and flexibility, make cloud computing appealing to companies of all kinds. But a problem known as the "cloud skills gap" has emerged as a result of the quick uptake of cloud computing. There is a scarcity of individuals in India who possess the necessary cloud skills to handle and use cloud technology efficiently, which is a problem for many enterprises. This essay will examine the causes of the skills gap in cloud computing in India and go over some approaches to close it.

Causes of India's Cloud Skills Gap

1. **Inadequate Training and Education Programs**
   A primary cause of the skills gap in cloud computing in India is the absence of appropriate educational and training initiatives. The majority of conventional educational establishments still do not include cloud computing in their curricula. Graduating students thus lack the expertise and understanding of cloud computing that businesses demand. Furthermore, the continuously changing nature of cloud technology may make it impossible for educational institutions, even those that do offer courses linked to it, to stay up, creating a skills gap with industry demand.

2. **Inadequate Knowledge and Awareness of Cloud Computing**
   The lack of awareness and comprehension of cloud computing among professionals, students, and even businesses is another factor contributing to the skills gap in the cloud. Since cloud computing is still a relatively new and complicated area, many people are unaware of its potential or how their organizations may benefit from it. The lack of knowledge deters people from pursuing employment in the cloud and prevents businesses from funding staff cloud training.

3. **Limited Supply and High Demand**

In India, there is a considerable need for professionals with cloud expertise but a very low supply. There is a dearth of skilled workers that can efficiently manage cloud infrastructure, create cloud solutions, and offer cloud support due to the market's rapid expansion. Organizations are competing more to draw and keep qualified cloud workers as a result of the strong demand and short supply.

Ways to Close the Skills Gap in Cloud Computing

1. **Encouraging Cloud Training and Education**

   In order to bridge the skills gap in cloud computing, cloud education and training initiatives must be supported in India. All levels of educational institutions, including colleges, universities, and schools, should include cloud computing in their curricula. Furthermore, training courses and certificates in a range of cloud technologies can be obtained through specialist cloud training institutions and online resources. Organizations may locate a bigger pool of eligible candidates and people can obtain the essential skills through increasing cloud education and training.

2. **Cooperation between Academic and Industry**

   To close the skills gap in the cloud, industry and academia must work together. To ensure that cloud-related curriculum represent the demands of the industry both now and in the future, industry experts can provide input into their creation. Additionally, they can offer students opportunities for internships, guest lectures, and on-the-job training so they can hone their cloud skills and obtain real-world experience. In a similar vein, academic institutions can work with business partners to provide access to real-world projects and case studies, providing students with practical cloud computing exposure.

3. **Financial Assistance and Incentive Programs**

   By offering incentives and support, the government can play a critical role in closing the skills gap in the cloud. This might include funding for cloud-related infrastructure development by educational institutions, subsidies for cloud technology research and development, and financial aid for professionals and students pursuing cloud certifications and training courses. Nationwide cloud awareness, education, and skill development can be aided by government programs.

4. Ongoing Education and Career Advancement

Cloud technology is changing quickly, and workers need to pursue ongoing education and professional development to stay up to date with market demands. It is recommended that people utilize webinars, conferences, workshops, and online learning environments in order to remain current on the newest developments in cloud computing. Additionally, companies ought to support their staff members' participation in training initiatives and offer opportunities for continued skill improvement.

For cloud computing to be successfully adopted and used, it is imperative that the skills gap in cloud computing be addressed in India. This disparity is exacerbated by a lack of appropriate education and training initiatives, a lack of knowledge of cloud computing, and a high demand relative to a low supply. Through the provision of government support, the encouragement of cloud education and training, industry-academia collaboration, and continuous learning, India can close the skills gap in cloud computing and produce a workforce capable of utilizing cloud technology to propel innovation, growth, and competitiveness in the global market.

7.2 Training and Upskilling Initiatives

The need of learning new skills and upgrading old ones cannot be overstated in the fast-paced, constantly-evolving employment environment of today. Certifications and credentials that formerly promised lifetime value are rapidly becoming out of date. People need to learn the skills needed to excel in their fields of expertise and adjust to the quickly evolving employment needs in order to stay competitive.

In-depth discussions of training and upskilling programs will be covered in this article, along with their advantages, necessity, and many approaches that people, groups, and governments can take to promote lifelong learning and ongoing upskilling.

Why Are Initiatives for Training and Upskilling Important?

1. **Adjust to the Development of Technology**
   Technological innovations like machine learning and artificial intelligence have affected every industry, changing the nature of work and creating new industries that need for a wide range of skill sets. Being technologically literate is becoming essential in today's environment, rather than optional. Initiatives for upskilling and training equip people for tasks requiring sophisticated technology, keeping them relevant and marketable in their industries.

2. **Fill in Skill Gaps**
   A skill gap arises when the workforce's skill set and the changing needs of jobs are not aligned. By offering specialized training programs to assist staff in gaining the skills they need to function more effectively within their firms, upskilling efforts seek to rectify this imbalance. By concentrating on skill gaps, companies can make sure that their talent pool is prepared to fulfill specific organizational needs, which lowers employee churn and improves output quality.

3. **Strengthen Engagement and Retention of Staff**

Initiatives for training and upskilling are also essential for improving employee engagement and retention. Workers who have a sense of ownership over their work are more likely to stick with them and feel like they belong in their companies. Employees who feel appreciated by their employers are also more open to accepting new jobs and responsibilities.

Advantages of Initiatives for Training and Upskilling

1. **Increased Contentment at Work**
   Individuals who participate in upskilling programs have the chance to learn new skills and take on new jobs, which increases job satisfaction. As workers advance in their positions, they get

greater satisfaction from their work, which lowers burnout and produces a highly motivated workforce.

2. **Decreased Rates of Turnover**

Programs for upskilling and training employees can lower employee turnover rates. Investments made show growth, and staff members are confident in their present positions and the possibility of advancement. Furthermore, workers who feel valued are less inclined to look for other alternatives.

3. **Enhanced Work Output**

Employee productivity is increased by upskilling programs because they enable workers to take on more difficult jobs and project responsibilities by expanding their skill and knowledge base. Increased productivity helps workers achieve better levels of job success and improves the quality of the work they do.

Techniques for Initiatives in Training and Upskilling

1. **Cooperation between Academic and Industry**

Collaborations between academic institutions and business give companies more chances to get the skills their workforce needs. Training programs must be specifically designed to meet the demands of businesses, offering a clearer balance between theory and practice. Academic institutions and business owners might collaborate to offer internships to students who are motivated to work on real-world projects. Employers who participate in curriculum creation give students the information and skills they need as well as a clear route to work following graduation.

2. **Government Assistance and Subsidies**

Governments everywhere have the ability to subsidize workers who want to participate in upskilling or training projects. Rewards play a critical role in promoting continuous growth and lifelong learning. Governments can also provide infrastructure and resources necessary for upskilling and short-term training programs, as well as funding for research, technological incubation centers, and innovation initiatives.

3. **Digital Channels**

Regardless of a person's location, schedule, or physical accessibility, online learning platforms are crucial in enabling access to learning opportunities. Because they are self-paced and asynchronous, online courses make it simpler to schedule learning around current obligations. People who reside in rural places or have limited access to educational facilities can benefit from having access to online learning tools, which are not limited by geography.

4. **Dedication to the Organization**

Employers ought to give their staff members a positive work atmosphere so they can succeed. Initiatives for upskilling should be seen as investments rather than expenses. The programs ought to be included in the training budgets rather than being an additional cost. It is also important to support and provide time off for employees to take part in these initiatives.

Initiatives for upskilling and training are crucial tactics for helping people and businesses stay competitive in the fast-paced labor market of today. These programs guarantee that employees have the abilities needed to succeed in their areas, empowering them to adapt to changing job demands and career goals. Programs for upskilling increase output, job satisfaction, and employee retention rates; these factors result in a more driven workforce, better corporate outcomes, and a healthier economy. The workforce needs to be upskilled, and some ways that can be used to meet those demands are encouraging lifelong learning, providing incentives, creating teamwork, and supporting continuous improvement.

7.3 Building Cloud-Ready Teams

Cloud computing technologies are being quickly adopted, which is causing big changes in the way businesses work today. Cloud computing has changed the way businesses work by providing unmatched scalability, freedom, and cost-effectiveness. As more and more businesses move their processes to the cloud, it becomes more and more important for teams to be ready for the cloud. These teams make sure that companies can use cloud technology to its fullest potential by driving innovation and the successful adoption of the cloud. This article will talk about the idea of "building cloud-ready teams," the most important skills and traits these teams should have, and the best ways to encourage and support them.

The Rise of the Cloud

1. **Being scalable:**
   Businesses don't have to worry about not having enough or too many cloud resources because they are easy to scale up or down to meet changing needs. This adaptability lets resources be used effectively and costs be kept as low as possible.

2. **Savings on costs:**
   Cloud computing lowers capital costs by getting rid of the need to buy and maintain devices up front. Cost-efficiency is improved because organizations only pay for the tools they use.

3. **Easy access:**
   The cloud lets people with an internet connection reach resources from afar. This makes it easier for people to work from home, collaborate, and help companies reach customers around the world.

4. **New ideas:**

There are a lot of tools and services for development, data analysis, and AI that can be found in the cloud. This encourages new ideas by giving companies the tools and facilities they need to create and use cutting-edge solutions.

Because of these benefits, more and more companies are moving their operations to the cloud, where they can do things like host their websites and run complex data analytics and machine learning tasks.

But if you want to successfully use cloud technologies, you need to do more than just set them up technically. You also need to build teams that are ready for the cloud.

What Do Cloud-Ready Teams Do?

Groups of people in an organization who have the skills, knowledge, and mindset to use cloud computing technologies successfully are called "cloud-ready teams." The people on these teams come from a lot of different departments, like IT, development, operations, security, and business planning. The goal is to make sure that the organization's goals and ideals are in line with the cloud adoption process as a whole.

Important Skills and Traits of Cloud-Ready Teams:

Expertise in the Cloud: Teams that are ready for the cloud should know a lot about systems like AWS, Azure, and Google Cloud. Members of the team should know a lot about infrastructure as code, cloud services, and best practices for cloud design.

Collaboration: It's important to be able to work together well because adopting the cloud often requires teams from different departments to work together. To reach their goals, members must talk to each other, share thoughts, and work together without any problems. Teams that are ready for the cloud need to be able to respond quickly to changes in technology and business needs. They should be able to change direction and come up with new ideas as things change.

Being aware of security: Safety should be your top concern. To protect data and apps well, team members need to know about cloud security principles and best practices.

Automation: Knowing how to use and program automation tools and methods is necessary to make cloud operations run more smoothly and cut down on manual work. Automation raises productivity and lowers the chance of mistakes made by people.

Cost Management: To make sure that cloud resources are used efficiently and cheaply, teams should know how to keep an eye on and improve cloud prices.

Learning All the Time: Cloud technology changes very quickly. Teams that are ready for the cloud need to have a mindset of always learning and getting better in order to keep up with the latest changes.

Tips for Making Teams Ready for the Cloud:

Assessment and Skill Gap Analysis: To begin, you should look at what skills and knowledge your company already has. Find skill gaps and places that need work to make a starting point.

Training and Certification: To help team members get better at using the cloud, spend money on training and certification programs. Cloud companies' certifications show that you know what you're doing and can be used to set standards for skill levels.

Cross-Functional Collaboration: Get the IT, development, management, and business teams to work together more. Get them to work on cloud projects together so you can see the effects of cloud usage as a whole.

Mentorship and Sharing of Knowledge: Put together team members who are new to cloud platforms with people who have experience with them. To speed up learning, encourage mentoring and sharing of information.

Hands-on Experience: Give people chances to use cloud tools in real life. This could be done in sandboxes or on real projects where team members can use what they've learned.

Continuous Feedback and Improvement: Set up a feedback loop to keep an eye on the team's work and help them do better. Ask people on the team to share what they've learned and what they think are the best ways to do things.

Leadership Buy-In: Get backing from top managers. Leaders should know how important it is for the business to use the cloud and push for the growth of teams that are ready to use it.

Governance in the Cloud: Use governance techniques in the cloud to make sure compliance, security, and cost management. Cloud governance models help keep things under control while still letting new ideas come up.

Community Involvement: Tell your team members to join cloud groups and forums. Making connections with people in the same line of work can give you useful information and help.To help you get started with the cloud, make sure you have clear, measurable goals. Check in on progress often and make changes to your plans as needed to reach your goals.

7.4 Collaborations with Educational Institutions

Businesses and schools working together has been known for a long time to be a powerful way to spur innovation, improve worker development, and move education forward. Partnerships like these are good for both sides. Businesses can use the talent, research skills, and new ideas that educational institutions offer, and universities can get access to real-world tools and applications. We will talk about the different aspects of working together with schools, the benefits they offer to both sides, and the best ways to make these relationships work.

Why working together is a good idea

1. **Getting Talent:**
   Schools, like universities, colleges, and trade schools, are where future stars are born. They get kids who are eager to learn, have the most up-to-date information and skills, and often really care about the subjects they choose. Businesses can use this group of talented people for jobs, co-op programs, and even hiring.

2. **Research and new ideas:**
   Universities are places where new ideas and study are born. Faculty members and students do cutting edge study in many fields, from business and the arts to science and technology. Businesses can use the study expertise of educational institutions to make new products, solve problems, and stay on the cutting edge of innovation by working with them.

3. **Taking part in the community:**
   Schools and colleges are important parts of the areas where they are located. Libraries, labs, and cultural centers are some of the

useful tools that they offer that businesses can use.

These places of business often do things to help the community and be socially responsible. This gives businesses chances to help with local growth and charity.

4. **Learning for life:**

In today's busy world, the idea of learning throughout life has become more popular. Businesses can benefit from schools because they give workers the chance to keep learning and improve their skills, which is very important in this age of fast technological change.

Good things for businesses

1. **Getting to new talent:**
   Businesses can find and hire bright students early in their lives through internships, co-op programs, and recruitment efforts. This keeps a steady flow of people who want to work for the company and already know how it works and what its values are.

2. **Research and new ideas:**
   Schools and colleges often have specialized study facilities and centers that can be used to help businesses solve tough problems. Working together on research projects can lead to new ideas that make a business more competitive.

3. **Info about the market:**
   Schools and colleges can give useful feedback on goods and services and market information. As customers, students can offer new ideas and points of view that could lead to better products or new business possibilities.

4. **Improving the brand:**

A company's brand image can be improved by forming partnerships with reputable schools. Being connected to academia shows a dedication to learning, study, and social responsibility, which can positively affect how people see you.

Relationships that last a long time:

When businesses work with schools, they often end up building long-term ties. When alumni go to work, they may still stay involved with their old school and, by extension, the business that works with them.

Advantages for schools and colleges

1. **Uses in the real world:**

   Collaborations give students chances to use what they've learned in the classroom in real life. This hands-on learning makes their schooling better and gets them ready for work better.

2. **Money and resources:**

   Partnerships with businesses can help schools get the money and tools they need. This help can be put into building up facilities, funding research, giving out scholarships, and helping teachers grow.

3. **Relevance and Improving the Curriculum:**

   By keeping in touch with businesses, schools can make sure that their classes are still useful to what the industry needs. This alignment makes it easier for graduates to find jobs and improves the school's image.

4. **Chances to do research:**

   Faculty members often get access to industry data, problems, and money for study projects when they work with businesses. This not only moves the institution's study agenda forward, but it also helps faculty grow.

5. **Networking and getting alumni involved:**

Collaborations can help both students and teachers meet new people and make connections. This interaction with professionals in the field can help students get internships, work together on study projects, and find jobs.

Strategies for Working Together Well

1. **Make your goals clear:**
   First, make a list of the exact goals of the collaboration. Set up key performance indicators to track progress and find out what both sides want to achieve.

2. **Find benefits for both sides:**
   You should make sure that the partnership is good for both the business and the school. A win-win method makes for a good partnership that lasts.

3. **Create well-organized plans:**
   Set up structured programs like co-op work, internships, and group study projects. These programs give people a way to get involved and make sure that the things they do are in line with the goals of the partnership.

4. **Improve communication:**
   Keep the lines of contact open and clear between both sides. Having regular meetings and ways for people to give feedback help deal with problems and make the connection stronger.

5. **Thoughts on the law and ethics:**
   Think about things that are moral and the law, like intellectual property rights, privacy, and sharing data. Set clear rules to make sure that everyone's interests are protected.

6. **Promise to be involved for a long time:**
   A long-term commitment is often needed for partnerships to work. You should be ready to put time, effort, and money into making the relationship last.

7. **Check and change:**
   Check in on the cooperation often, and be ready to change your plans based on what you find. To get the most out of the relationship, it's important to keep getting better.

8. **Get Stakeholders Involved:**

Key people from both the business and the school should be involved in the teamwork. Stakeholders who are involved are more likely to support the partnership and make sure it works.

Examples from real life

1. **Partnerships for research:**
   A drug company and a university's biology department work together to look into possible solutions for a rare disease. The company's means and knowledge in drug development are combined with the university's research skills in this partnership.

2. **Programs for internships:**
   A car company works with a technical college to give students learning automotive engineering the chance to do internships. Internships like these give students real-world experience and help the company find people who might become future workers.

3. **Incubators for entrepreneurs:**
   A tech company helps fund a center for new businesses at a nearby college. This program helps aspiring student entrepreneurs by giving them money, advice, and other tools. It also encourages new ideas and possible business partnerships.

4. **Developing the workforce:**

A business group in the area works with community schools in the area to create customized programs for training the workforce. These programs help meet the special skill needs of businesses in the area, which makes sure that the workforce is well-trained.

Chapter 8

Overcoming Challenges and Pitfalls

Life is an excursion loaded up with exciting bends in the road, ups and downs, and a bunch of difficulties and entanglements en route. Regardless of whether we like it, misfortune is an unavoidable piece of the human experience. Notwithstanding, it is the means by which we answer these difficulties and traps that eventually characterizes the course of our lives. In this far reaching investigation, we will dive into the different parts of defeating difficulties and traps, offering bits of knowledge, systems, and genuine guides to direct us on this frequently turbulent in any case groundbreaking excursion.

Presentation

Difficulties and traps are a necessary piece of the human condition. They come in different structures, going from individual battles like medical problems, monetary misfortunes, and relationship issues to cultural difficulties like segregation, financial emergencies, and ecological issues. While these difficulties can be overwhelming, they likewise present open doors for development, versatility, and self-improvement.

The Significance of Flexibility

Flexibility is the capacity to return from affliction and adjust to new conditions. A vital quality enables people to confront life's difficulties with mental fortitude and determination. Versatile people recuperate from difficulties as well as use them as venturing stones to become more grounded, more caring, and more creative.

The Job of Mentality

One's mentality assumes a critical part in defeating difficulties. A development outlook, which is the conviction that capacities and knowledge can be created through commitment and difficult work, can enable people to persist through hardships. On the other hand, a proper outlook, which expects that capacities are intrinsic and unchangeable, can impede progress.

Individual Difficulties and Entanglements

Wellbeing Difficulties

1. **Constant Diseases:**
   Living with a constant sickness can be truly and genuinely burdening. It expects people to explore the intricacies of dealing with their wellbeing while at the same time keeping a feeling of predictability in their lives.

2. **Emotional well-being Battles:**

Emotional well-being issues, like sorrow and tension, can be undetectable yet profoundly effective. Conquering these difficulties frequently includes looking for proficient assistance, constructing an emotionally supportive network, and embracing methods for dealing with stress.

Monetary Difficulties

1. **Obligation and Monetary Difficulty:**
   Obligation and monetary battles can prompt pressure, tension, and a sensation of being caught. Methodologies for beating monetary difficulties incorporate planning, looking for monetary guidance, and investigating obligation help choices.

2. Joblessness:

Losing an employment can be a critical difficulty, influencing not exclusively one's monetary steadiness yet in addition their confidence and feeling of direction. Work searchers frequently need to foster new abilities, organization, and persist through dismissal.

Relationship Issues

1. **Family Clashes:**
   Clashes inside families can sincerely deplete. Successful correspondence, compassion, and looking for proficient intervention are fundamental for settling family issues.
2. **Separations and Separation:**

The conclusion of a huge friendship can genuinely demolish. Recuperating and pushing ahead may include self-reflection, directing, and revamping one's life.

Individual Misfortune

1. **Distress and Mourning:**
   Losing a friend or family member is quite possibly of life's most significant test. Lamenting is a one of a kind cycle for every person, and it is crucial for look for help and permit oneself to grieve in their own particular manner.
2. **Loss of Direction:**

Feeling uncontrolled or coming up short on a feeling of direction can be an individual entanglement. Rediscovering reason frequently includes self-revelation, laying out significant objectives, and investigating new interests.

Cultural Difficulties and Traps

Separation and Imbalance

1. **Racial and Ethnic Separation:**
   Racial and ethnic separation can have sweeping outcomes on people and networks. Conquering these difficulties requires aggregate endeavors to advance inclusivity and civil rights.
2. **Orientation Disparity:**

Orientation based separation and disparity continue in numerous social orders. Promotion, training, and strategy changes are fundamental in resolving these issues.

Monetary Emergencies

1. **Employment Cutback during Monetary Slumps:**
   Monetary downturns and emergencies can prompt broad employment cutback. Survival techniques incorporate gaining new abilities, changing ways of managing money, and looking for government help.
2. **Pay Disparity:**

Tending to pay disparity includes pushing for fair wages, admittance to training, and social security nets to help those out of luck.

Ecological Difficulties

1. **Environmental Change:**
   Environmental change represents a worldwide danger with sweeping outcomes. People can contribute by taking on feasible works on, supporting natural drives, and pushing for environment activity.
2. **Cataclysmic events:**

Cataclysmic events, like typhoons, seismic tremors, and out of control fires, can annihilate networks. Readiness, people group backing, and calamity aid projects are basic in their result.

Techniques for Defeating Difficulties and Traps

1. **Look for Help:**
   Individual Help:
   Contact companions, family, or an encouraging group of people. Discussing difficulties can mitigate close to home weights and give important viewpoints.
   Proficient Help:
   Think about looking for help from specialists, advisors, or care groups. Experts can offer direction and procedures for adapting to explicit difficulties.

2. **Foster Strength:**
   Develop a Development Mentality:
   Have confidence in your capacity to learn, adjust, and develop. Embrace difficulties as any open doors for self-improvement.
   Practice Taking care of oneself:
   Focus on taking care of oneself exercises that advance physical and mental prosperity, like activity, reflection, and care.

3. **Put forth Reasonable Objectives:**
   Break Difficulties into More modest Advances:
   Partition huge difficulties into sensible errands to try not to feel overpowered.
   Make an Arrangement:
   Foster a substantial arrangement for tending to difficulties, including explicit objectives, cutoff times, and activity steps.

4. **Gain from Difficulties:**
   Embrace Disappointment:
   Disappointment is much of the time a venturing stone to progress. Investigate what turned out badly, change your methodology, and continue.
   Foster Critical thinking Abilities:
   Improve your capacity to distinguish arrangements and adjust to evolving conditions.

5. **Fabricate a Strong People group:**
   Associate with Similar People:

Join gatherings, associations, or networks that share your inclinations and values.

Offer in return:

Support other people who are confronting difficulties. Thoughtful gestures can make a positive expanding influence.

6. **Center around Self-Empathy:**

Be Thoughtful to Yourself:

Stay away from self-analysis and practice self-empathy. Indulge yourself with a similar generosity you would offer a companion experiencing the same thing.

7. **Remain Educated and Locked in:**

Backing:

Participate in support endeavors connected with cultural difficulties. Support strategies and drives that line up with your qualities.

Deep rooted Learning:

Ceaselessly secure information and abilities to adjust to changing conditions and remain informed about worldwide difficulties.

Genuine Instances of Defeating Difficulties

1. **Malala Yousafzai - Promoter for Young ladies' Schooling:**

   Malala Yousafzai, a Pakistani dissident, confronted outrageous misfortune when she was designated by the Taliban for supporting young ladies' schooling.

   In spite of being shot in the head, she made due as well as kept on advocating the reason for schooling for young ladies around the world. Her strength and support prompted her turning into the most youthful ever Nobel Prize laureate.

2. **Elon Musk - Business visionary and Trend-setter:**

   Elon Musk, the President of Tesla and SpaceX, experienced various difficulties and monetary difficulties all through his vocation. Regardless of confronting numerous business disappointments and individual battles, he endured and turned into a trailblazer in the electric vehicle and space investigation enterprises.

3. **Nelson Mandela - Against Politically-sanctioned racial segregation Pioneer:**
Nelson Mandela burned through 27 years in jail for his job in the counter politically-sanctioned racial segregation battle in South Africa. Upon his delivery, he worked enthusiastically to end politically-sanctioned racial segregation and turned into the nation's most memorable dark president. His obligation to pardoning and compromise exemplified the force of versatility and assurance.

4. **J.K. Rowling - Top rated Creator:**

Prior to accomplishing global notoriety as the creator of the Harry Potter series, J.K. Rowling confronted individual difficulties, including neediness and melancholy. Her tirelessness and commitment to composing ultimately prompted the production of perhaps of the most cherished scholarly establishment ever.

Life is an excursion full of difficulties and traps, however it is likewise overflowing with potential open doors for development, change, and flexibility. By taking on a development mentality, looking for help, laying out reasonable objectives, and gaining from misfortune, people can beat individual difficulties. Besides, by remaining informed, supporting for change, and drawing in with networks, we can all in all address cultural difficulties and make an additional evenhanded and reasonable world.

In the expressions of Maya Angelou, "You might experience many losses, however you should not be crushed. As a matter of fact, it could be important to experience the losses so you can know what your identity is, what you can ascend from, how you can in any case emerge from it." Embracing difficulties and entanglements isn't just a demonstration of our solidarity yet in addition a potential chance to manufacture a way towards a more splendid and stronger future.

8.1 Common Challenges in Cloud Adoption

Distributed computing has changed the manner in which organizations work, offering versatility, cost-productivity, and nimbleness more than ever. Be that as it may, the excursion to cloud reception isn't without its difficulties. Associations setting out on this way frequently experience different obstructions that require cautious preparation, procedure, and execution to survive. In this article, we will investigate a portion of the normal difficulties in cloud reception and give systems to organizations to effectively explore these obstacles.

The Developing Meaning of Cloud Reception

Adaptability: Cloud assets can be increased or down in view of interest, guaranteeing productive asset distribution.

Cost-Effectiveness: Distributed computing lessens the requirement for forthright equipment ventures and upkeep costs, permitting associations to pay just for what they use.

Adaptability: The cloud empowers remote admittance to assets, cultivating joint effort and remote work abilities.

Advancement: Cloud suppliers offer a rich biological system of instruments and administrations, working with the turn of events and sending of state of the art arrangements, for example, man-made intelligence and AI.In any case, as associations leave on their cloud reception ventures, they frequently experience normal moves that should be tended to in a calculated manner.

Normal Difficulties in Cloud Reception

1. **Security Concerns:**

   Security is a top worry for associations thinking about cloud reception. Putting away information and applications in the cloud implies giving up some command over actual security, which can raise anxieties about information breaks, unapproved access, and consistence with information assurance guidelines.

   Procedure:

   Direct an extensive gamble evaluation to recognize potential security weaknesses.

Carry out vigorous safety efforts, including encryption, access controls, and multifaceted validation.

Pick a cloud supplier with a solid security history and consistence confirmations.

2. **Consistence and Information Protection:**

Numerous businesses are dependent upon severe administrative necessities with respect to information taking care of and protection. Guaranteeing consistence with these guidelines while moving information to the cloud can challenge.

Procedure:

Comprehend the particular consistence necessities applicable to your industry and locale.

Work with legitimate and consistence specialists to think up a consistence technique for cloud reception.

Pick a cloud supplier that offers consistence certificates and instruments to assist with adherence.

3. **Information Movement Difficulties:**

Moving existing information and applications to the cloud can be intricate, tedious, and blunder inclined. Similarity issues, information move bottlenecks, and personal time concerns are normal difficulties.

Methodology:

Plan the relocation cycle carefully, taking into account factors like information volume, conditions, and booking.

Use movement apparatuses and administrations given by cloud suppliers to rearrange and mechanize the cycle.

Perform careful testing and approval when movement to limit disturbances.

4. **Cost Administration:**

While cloud reception can decrease framework costs, it can likewise present new expense difficulties. Associations might battle to screen and control cloud spending actually, prompting surprising costs.

Technique:

Carry out cost administration apparatuses and practices to follow cloud spending and recognize cost-saving open doors.

Put forth financial plan lines and alarms to forestall cost overwhelms.

Consistently audit and upgrade cloud assets to guarantee cost-effectiveness.

5. **Absence of Cloud Ability:**

Changing to the cloud requires a gifted labor force with mastery in cloud advancements, which numerous associations might need at first.

System:

Put resources into cloud preparing and accreditation programs for IT staff and representatives.

Consider recruiting cloud specialists or joining forces with cloud counseling firms to fill ability holes.

Encourage a culture of constant learning and information sharing inside the association.

6. **Merchant Lock-In:**

Picking a specific cloud supplier can prompt merchant secure in, making it trying to change to one more supplier or get administrations back house.

Procedure:

Embrace a multi-cloud or mixture cloud methodology to relieve seller secure in chances.

Utilize normalized, open-source innovations and containerization to increment transportability.

Arrange leave methodologies with cloud suppliers on the off chance that you really want to change away from their administrations.

7. **Execution and Idleness Issues:**

The exhibition of cloud administrations can be affected by factors like organization dormancy and the geographic area of server farms, which can influence client experience.

System:

Select cloud areas and server farms decisively to limit dormancy.

Utilize content conveyance organizations (CDNs) to improve content conveyance and diminish inertness.

Screen and tweak cloud assets to consistently improve execution.

8. **Change The board and Culture Shift:**

Cloud reception frequently requires a social shift inside an association. Protection from change, feeling of dread toward work removal, and newness to cloud advances can obstruct progress.

Methodology:

Impart the advantages and reasoning for cloud reception obviously to all partners.

Give preparing and backing to representatives to assist them with adjusting to new advances and work processes.

Empower a culture of development and dexterity that embraces change for of progress.

Genuine Instances of Effective Cloud Reception

1. **Netflix - Versatility and Cost Administration:**
   Netflix, a worldwide streaming stage, effectively tended to the test of versatility and cost administration by taking on a cloud-local methodology. They depend on Amazon Web Administrations (AWS) for their foundation needs, empowering them to increase to serve a great many watchers during top use while effectively overseeing costs through asset streamlining.

2. **Capital One - Security and Consistence:**
   Capital One, a monetary foundation, embraced the cloud while keeping up with rigid security and consistence norms. They laid out an exhaustive security program, including personality and access the executives (IAM), encryption, and nonstop checking,

to safeguard client information and guarantee consistence with monetary guidelines.

3. General Electric (GE) - Merchant Lock-In Alleviation:

GE embraced a multi-cloud system to relieve seller secure in chances. By using different cloud suppliers, including AWS, Microsoft Purplish blue, and others, they kept up with adaptability and the capacity to pick the best-fit cloud administrations for different specialty units while keeping away from complete reliance on a solitary seller.

Cloud reception is an extraordinary excursion that offers various advantages yet in addition presents different difficulties. By getting it and tending to these normal difficulties decisively, associations can prepare for effective cloud reception and progressing improvement of cloud assets.

Security concerns can be alleviated through powerful measures, consistence with administrative necessities can be guaranteed, and information relocation difficulties can be overwhelmed with cautious preparation. Viable expense the executives, labor force improvement, and social movements can likewise add to a smoother progress to the cloud.

Eventually, effective cloud reception isn't just about innovation; about embracing an all encompassing methodology consolidates specialized skill, hierarchical preparation, and a guarantee to adjust and fill in a quickly developing computerized scene. With the right procedures and a reasonable vision, associations can tackle the force of the cloud to drive development, improve dexterity, and accomplish their business targets.

8.2 Strategies for Mitigating Risks

Endanger is an innate piece of life and business. Whether you're running an organization, putting resources into stocks, or leaving on another experience, there are consistently vulnerabilities and possible traps to fight with. Nonetheless, the way to long haul achievement lies not in staying away from gambles by and large yet in figuring out them, overseeing them really, and moderating their expected adverse consequences. In this article, we will dive into the idea of chance relief, investigate normal gamble factors, and talk about techniques to defend your undertakings.

Grasping Gamble Relief

Risk alleviation is the method involved with distinguishing, evaluating, and going to proactive lengths to lessen the probability or effect of expected dangers and vulnerabilities. It is an essential part of chance administration, which expects to safeguard resources, speculations, projects, and, eventually, the accomplishment of objectives and goals.

Viable gamble relief procedures include a blend of preventive measures, possibility arranging, and hazard move components to guarantee that the effect of unfriendly occasions is limited. These methodologies can be applied to different spaces, including business, finance, project the board, and individual independent direction.

Normal Gamble Elements

1. **Monetary Gamble:**
   Market Hazard: Vacillations in monetary business sectors can affect speculations and portfolios.
   Credit Chance: Default by borrowers or counterparties can prompt monetary misfortunes.
   Liquidity Hazard: Lacking income can impede tasks and dissolvability.
2. **Functional Gamble:**
   Human Blunder: Mix-ups made by representatives or the board can bring about functional disappointments.
   Innovative Disappointments: Framework blackouts, network protection breaks, and IT errors can disturb tasks.
   Store network Disturbances: Postponements or disturbances in the store network can influence creation and conveyance.
3. **Reputational Chance:**
   Negative Exposure: Embarrassments, contentions, or negative

client encounters can hurt an association's standing.

Brand Harm: A harmed brand can prompt loss of trust and client dependability.

4. **Project Chance:**
   Tasks running amok: Extending project scope without appropriate arranging can prompt postponements and financial plan invades.

   Asset Deficiencies: Insufficient assets can upset project execution.

   Administrative Changes: Developing guidelines can affect project consistence.

5. **Ecological and Cataclysmic event Hazard:**
   Cataclysmic events: Quakes, storms, floods, and out of control fires can cause property harm and business interruptions.

   Natural Guidelines: Consistence with ecological regulations and guidelines is fundamental to stay away from lawful and reputational chances.

6. **Individual Gamble:**

Wellbeing Dangers: Ailments or mishaps can prompt clinical costs and lost pay.

Vocation Dangers: Employment misfortune or profession difficulties can influence monetary solidness and individual objectives.

Systems for Alleviating Dangers

1. **Risk Distinguishing proof and Appraisal:**
   Recognize Dangers: Start by distinguishing expected dangers and vulnerabilities pertinent to your specific situation, whether in business, money, or individual life.

   Survey Effect and Probability: Assess the expected effect of each gamble and its probability happening. This focuses on relief endeavors.

2. **Enhancement:**

   Monetary Enhancement: Spread speculations across different resource classes to lessen openness to advertise unpredictability.

   Provider Expansion: Work with different providers to limit the effect of store network disturbances.

   Ability Broadening: Fabricate a different and gifted labor force to relieve functional and progression chances.

3. **Protection and Hazard Move:**

   Buy Protection: Get fitting protection inclusion to safeguard against monetary misfortunes connected with wellbeing, property, and business tasks.

   Authoritative Arrangements: Use agreements and arrangements that allot risk fittingly among parties, like reimbursement provisos.

4. **Possibility Arranging:**

   Foster Alternate courses of action: Get ready alternate courses of action that frame reactions to explicit dangers. These plans can assist with limiting margin time and misfortunes if there should be an occurrence of unanticipated occasions.

   Business Progression Arranging: Lay out techniques for keeping up with fundamental business activities during interruptions.

5. **A reasonable level of investment and Exploration:**

   Lead An expected level of effort: Completely research likely speculations, accomplices, and undertakings to recognize stowed away dangers.

   Remain Informed: Stay up to date with industry patterns, economic situations, and administrative changes that could affect your undertakings.

6. **Risk Moderation Financial plan:**

   Designate Assets: Put away assets, both monetary and human, for risk relief exercises.

   Focus on Relief Endeavors: Designate assets in view of the criticality and probability of dangers.

7. **Representative Preparation and Mindfulness:**
Train Workers: Give representatives preparing and assets to recognize and address functional dangers.
Cultivate a Gamble Mindful Culture: Urge representatives to report expected dangers and prize proactive gamble the board.

8. **Situation Arranging:**
Situation Examination: Foster situations that investigate different gamble results and their suggestions. This aides in planning for various potential outcomes.
Stress Testing: Stress-test monetary models and tasks to evaluate flexibility in unfavorable circumstances.

9. **Ordinary Audit and Variation:**
Constant Observing: Consistently audit and update risk evaluations to represent changing conditions and arising gambles.
Adjust Systems: Change risk alleviation procedures depending on the situation in light of new data and illustrations learned.

10. **Lawful and Administrative Consistence:**

vbnet
Duplicate code
Legitimate Advice: Counsel legitimate specialists to guarantee consistence with regulations and guidelines pertinent to your industry.
Risk Evaluation for Consistence: Direct gamble appraisals to recognize consistence chances and foster relief plans.
Genuine Instances of Chance Alleviation

1. **SpaceX - Possibility Arranging and Expansion:**
SpaceX, the aviation producer and space transportation organization, is known for its possibility arranging and expansion endeavors. In space investigation, where dangers are inborn, SpaceX's methodology remembers overt repetitiveness for frameworks, alternate courses of action for mission disappointments,

and a different arrangement of missions, including satellite send-offs and ran missions to the Worldwide Space Station.

2. **Speculation Portfolios - Enhancement:**
   Speculation portfolios ordinarily utilize broadening procedures to moderate monetary gamble. Financial backers spread their resources across different resource classes, like stocks, bonds, and land, to lessen openness to the instability of any single venture.

3. **Medical services Organizations - Hazard Move (Protection):**

Medical services foundations, including clinics and clinical practices, depend on protection to alleviate takes a chance with connected with clinical negligence, patient wounds, and property harm. Clinical misbehavior protection, for instance, gives assurance if there should arise an occurrence of clinical mistakes and carelessness claims.

Endanger is a fundamental piece of life and business, however it doesn't need to be an obstruction to progress. By getting it, surveying, and proactively moderating dangers through a blend of techniques, people and associations can explore vulnerability with more noteworthy certainty. Whether it's monetary, functional, reputational, or individual gamble, a thoroughly examined risk relief plan can assist with protecting interests and save long haul objectives.

The way to powerful take a chance with moderation is to see it as a continuous interaction, not a one-time exertion. Consistently survey gambles, adjust methodologies, and remain informed to guarantee that your gamble relief endeavors stay compelling in an always impacting world. Eventually, risk relief is a vital component of capable navigation and reasonable administration in both individual and expert undertakings.

8.3 Avoiding Common Pitfalls

In the excursion towards accomplishing our objectives, whether they are private or expert, we frequently experience various snags and difficulties. These obstacles can once in a while lead us into normal entanglements that upset our advancement and even crash our endeavors.

In this investigation, we will dig into the absolute most common traps individuals face and, all the more critically, talk about methodologies to keep away from them.

Absence of Clear Objectives

Quite possibly of the most widely recognized trap people experience is the shortfall of clear, obvious objectives. Without a reasonable objective as a top priority, it's not difficult to capriciously get derailed or float. To stay away from this trap, begin by setting Shrewd (Explicit, Quantifiable, Feasible, Important, Time-bound) objectives. These objectives give a reasonable system and course for your endeavors.

Stalling

Stalling is the adversary of progress. It's amazingly simple to put off errands, especially those that are testing or less charming. To keep away from this entanglement, develop discipline, focus on undertakings, and break them into more modest, reasonable advances. Furthermore, lay out cutoff times and consider yourself responsible.

Absence of Arranging

Arranging is a pivotal part of accomplishing any objective. Skirting the arranging stage can prompt tumult and failure. To keep away from this trap, make a definite arrangement that frames the means expected to arrive at your objectives. Audit and change your arrangement as the need might arise, and be available to adjusting to unanticipated conditions.

Apprehension about Disappointment

Apprehension about disappointment can incapacitate. It frequently keeps people from facing challenges and chasing after their fantasies. To defeat this trap, shift your point of view on disappointment. Rather than survey it as a difficulty, think of it as an important opportunity for growth. Embrace disappointment as a venturing stone towards progress.

Overcommitment

Being excessively energetic and taking on such a large number of responsibilities can prompt burnout and diminished efficiency. To keep away from this entanglement, figure out how to say no when vital and focus on your significant investment on exercises that line up with your objectives.

Absence of Self-control

Self-restraint is a foundation of progress. Without it, you might battle to keep on track and reliably pursue your targets. To keep away from this entanglement, foster propensities and schedules that encourage self-control. Establish a helpful climate for efficiency and practice care to remain focused.

Negative Self-Talk

Negative self-talk can be an inevitable outcome. Accepting you can't accomplish your objectives can turn into a significant detour. To stay away from this entanglement, develop a positive mentality and practice self-sympathy. Supplant negative contemplations with insistences that engage and spur you.

Hairsplitting

While taking a stab at greatness is splendid, compulsiveness can incapacitate. It frequently prompts superfluous pressure and defers in the works. To keep away from this trap, perceive that flawlessness is impossible and spotlight on giving your all things considered. Acknowledge that missteps are essential for the educational experience.

Absence of Versatility

Unbending nature can ruin your advancement, particularly when confronted with unforeseen difficulties or evolving conditions. To stay away from this entanglement, develop versatility. Embrace change, be available to novel thoughts, and change your systems on a case by case basis.

Not Looking for Help

Pride or a feeling of dread toward seeming powerless can keep people from looking for help when they need it. To stay away from this entanglement, perceive that looking for help is an indication of solidarity, not shortcoming. Connect with coaches, companions, or specialists who can give direction and backing on your excursion.

Overlooking Criticism

Criticism is an important wellspring of knowledge and improvement. Disregarding or excusing criticism can obstruct your development and progress. To keep away from this entanglement, effectively look for input from others and be available to useful analysis. Use criticism as an instrument for personal development.

Absence of Persistence

Accomplishing huge objectives frequently takes time and determination. Anxiety can prompt disappointment and untimely surrender of your endeavors. To keep away from this trap, practice persistence and advise yourself that achievement is a long distance race, not a run.

Staying away from normal entanglements is fundamental on the way to progress. By defining clear objectives, conquering lingering, arranging successfully, embracing disappointment, rehearsing self-restraint, keeping a positive mentality, relinquishing hairsplitting, remaining versatile, looking for help while required, esteeming input, and rehearsing persistence, you can explore your excursion all the more easily. Recollect that achievement isn't the shortfall of hindrances yet the capacity to conquer them. In light of these procedures, you can defeat normal traps and keep gaining ground towards your objectives.

8.4 Best Practices for Cloud Governance

The reception of distributed computing has changed the manner in which associations work and deal with their IT assets. Cloud administrations offer unmatched adaptability, versatility, and cost-viability. In any case, they likewise present remarkable difficulties, especially regarding administration and security. To bridle the maximum capacity of the cloud while relieving gambles, associations should lay out hearty cloud administration rehearses. In this investigation, we will dig into the accepted procedures for cloud administration to guarantee security and productivity in the cloud.

Characterize Clear Goals and Arrangements

Viable cloud administration begins with characterizing clear goals and approaches. Start by understanding your association's essential objectives and how cloud reception lines up with them. Lay out obvious strategies that frame allowable cloud utilization, security conventions, consistence necessities, and information the executives rehearses. Guarantee these strategies are conveyed across the association.

Carry out Job Based Admittance Control (RBAC)

Job Based Admittance Control (RBAC) is vital for keeping up with security and consistence in the cloud. Dole out consents in light of occupation jobs, allowing just the essential admittance to people or groups. Routinely audit and update consents as jobs advance, and repudiate pointless access speedily to diminish the gamble of unapproved exercises.

Screen and Review Cloud Assets

Ceaseless checking and examining of cloud assets are fundamental for distinguishing and tending to security weaknesses and consistence issues. Use cloud-local apparatuses or outsider answers for screen asset usage, access logs, and setups. Carry out computerized cautions to instantly recognize and answer dubious exercises.

Execute Cloud Cost Administration

Cost administration is a basic part of cloud administration. Without legitimate oversight, cloud costs can twisting wild. Lay out cost administration rehearses, for example, setting financial plans, utilizing cost portion labels, and routinely inspecting utilization and spending reports. Improve asset allotment to decrease superfluous costs.

Embrace DevSecOps Standards

DevSecOps coordinates security rehearses into the DevOps pipeline, guaranteeing that security is a key piece of the turn of events and organization process. Consolidate security examining, weakness evaluations, and code investigation into your CI/Disc (Consistent Mix/Nonstop Organization) pipeline. Computerize security checks to distinguish and resolve gives from the get-go in the advancement cycle.

Scramble Information Very still and On the way

Information security is foremost in the cloud. Scramble delicate information both very still and on the way. Cloud suppliers offer encryption administrations, like AWS Key Administration (KMS) and Sky blue Key Vault, to oversee encryption keys safely. Guarantee that encryption conventions are utilized reliably for information assurance.

Lay out a Cloud Focus of Greatness (CCoE)

A Cloud Focus of Greatness (CCoE) is a committed group liable for overseeing cloud reception and tasks. This group ought to comprise of specialists in cloud engineering, security, consistence, and cost administration. The CCoE guides cloud drives, sets best practices, and works with information sharing across the association.

Execute Cloud Security Best Practices

Cloud security ought to be a main concern. Carry out cloud security best practices, like organization division, character and access the executives (IAM), multifaceted confirmation (MFA), and the rule of least honor (PoLP). Consistently survey your security stance and direct entrance testing to recognize weaknesses.

Mechanize Consistence Checks

Consistence with industry guidelines and inner arrangements is non-debatable, particularly for associations in profoundly controlled areas. Robotize consistence checks with guarantee that cloud assets comply to the fundamental guidelines and guidelines. Influence consistence as code (CaC) structures to uphold strategies through mechanization.

Reinforcement and Catastrophe Recuperation

Information misfortune and margin time can be horrendous for any association. Carry out powerful reinforcement and debacle recuperation (DR) systems in the cloud. Consistently back up basic information and applications, and test your DR plan to guarantee fast recuperation in case of a debacle.

Teach and Train Groups

Cloud administration is an aggregate exertion that includes all groups and people working with cloud assets. Give preparing and training projects to bring issues to light of cloud administration best practices. Cultivate a culture of safety and consistence by guaranteeing that all workers comprehend their job in keeping up with cloud administration.

Consistently Survey and Update Approaches

Cloud administration is certainly not a one-time exertion yet a continuous cycle. Routinely survey and update your cloud administration approaches to adjust to advancing advancements, business necessities, and administrative changes. Guarantee that your administration system stays lined up with your association's objectives.

Viable cloud administration is fundamental for associations hoping to saddle the advantages of distributed computing while at the same time alleviating chances. By characterizing clear targets and strategies, carrying out job based admittance control, observing and examining assets, embracing DevSecOps standards, scrambling information, laying out a Cloud Focal point of Greatness, and robotizing consistence checks, associations can explore the perplexing scene of cloud administration effectively. Besides, focusing on cloud security, cost administration, reinforcement and fiasco recuperation, and progressing training and strategy survey will guarantee that your cloud climate stays secure, proficient, and lined up with your business goals. Cloud administration is certainly not a one-size-fits-all methodology; it requires consistent assessment and transformation to satisfy the steadily changing needs of distributed computing in the present computerized age.

Chapter 9

Future Trends and Predictions

Foreseeing what's in store is a difficult undertaking, however one dazzles our aggregate creative mind. As we stand on the cusp of another period, set apart by fast innovative progressions, cultural movements, and ecological worries, thinking about what's on the horizon is just normal. In this investigation, we will dive into a large number of future patterns and forecasts across different spaces, including innovation, economy, medical care, climate, and society.

1. **Innovative Headways**
   Computerized reasoning and Computerization: Man-made consciousness (simulated intelligence) and robotization will keep on reshaping ventures and labor forces. Simulated intelligence driven navigation, advanced mechanics, and independent frameworks will turn out to be more common, prompting expanded proficiency and efficiency in different areas.
   Quantum Figuring: Quantum registering vows to upset processing power. It will open additional opportunities in fields like cryptography, materials science, and medication revelation,

tackling issues that were already computationally infeasible.

5G and Then some: The rollout of 5G organizations will empower quicker and more dependable remote correspondence, making ready for the Web of Things (IoT) to prosper. Past 5G, we can anticipate further headways in remote innovation, for example, 6G, which will offer considerably higher information rates and lower idleness.

Blockchain and Decentralization: Blockchain innovation will keep on upsetting businesses past cryptographic forms of money. Its applications in store network the board, casting a ballot frameworks, and medical services will build up some decent forward momentum, prompting expanded straightforwardness and security.

Space Investigation: Privately owned businesses like SpaceX and Blue Beginning are ready to assume a huge part in space investigation. The colonization of Mars, lunar natural surroundings, and space rock mining are conceivable outcomes not too far off.

2. **Monetary Movements**

   Advanced Monetary forms: National bank computerized monetary standards (CBDCs) and digital currencies will reshape the monetary scene. They could offer more prominent monetary consideration and decrease grating in cross-line exchanges.

   Gig Economy and Remote Work: The gig economy will extend, driven by a developing number of specialists and telecommuters. This shift might prompt changes in labor regulations and social security nets.

   Reasonable Strategic policies: Ecological and social obligation will become key to plans of action. Organizations will progressively embrace reasonable practices and adjust their tasks to the Assembled Countries' Manageable Improvement Objectives.

   Financial Imbalance: Tending to monetary disparity will be a major problem. Legislatures and associations should execute arrangements that advance fair abundance conveyance.

Advanced Change: Organizations will speed up their computerized change endeavors, with distributed computing, huge information examination, and online protection assuming crucial parts in guaranteeing seriousness.

3. **Medical care and Medication**

Customized Medication: Advances in genomics and information examination will empower the broad reception of customized medication. Medicines custom-made to a person's hereditary cosmetics will turn out to be more normal.

Telemedicine and Distant Wellbeing Checking: Telemedicine will proceed to grow, and far off wellbeing observing gadgets will turn out to be more complex, giving opportune medical care administrations and lessening the weight on customary medical services frameworks.

Man-made intelligence in Medical care: Computerized reasoning will be coordinated into medical care frameworks for undertakings like sickness conclusion, drug disclosure, and prescient examination, working on quiet results and decreasing expenses.

Regenerative Medication: Undeveloped cell research and regenerative medication will progress, possibly offering answers for conditions that were once viewed as serious.

Emotional wellness Mindfulness: Cultural attention to psychological well-being will build, prompting more prominent acknowledgment, better admittance to emotional wellness administrations, and destigmatization.

4. **Ecological Worries**

Environmental Change Moderation: The battle against environmental change will heighten. State run administrations, organizations, and people will put resources into environmentally friendly power, economical agribusiness, and carbon catch advances.

Biodiversity Preservation: Endeavors to safeguard and reestablish biodiversity will pick up speed. Protection practices and living space reclamation ventures will turn out to be more broad.

Roundabout Economy: The reception of a roundabout economy model, which underscores reusing, reusing, and diminishing waste, will increment, lessening asset utilization and natural effect.

Electric and Independent Vehicles: The change to electric and independent vehicles will speed up, decreasing ozone harming substance outflows and reforming transportation frameworks.

Green Innovation: Interests in green innovation, like clean energy, feasible materials, and eco-accommodating framework, will drive financial development and natural maintainability.

5. **Cultural Changes**

Segment Changes: Maturing populaces and declining rates of birth in numerous nations will reshape socioeconomics and influence medical services frameworks, retirement plans, and work markets.

Advanced Protection and Morals: Worries about computerized security and morals will develop. Regulation and guidelines will arise to safeguard people's information and guarantee moral utilization of innovation.

Instruction Development: Conventional schooling models will advance, with internet learning, ability based preparing, and deep rooted picking up acquiring unmistakable quality.

Social Movements: Social standards and values will keep on advancing, reflecting changing mentalities towards issues like orientation uniformity, variety, and civil rights.

Globalization and Patriotism: The pressure among globalization and patriotism will endure, impacting worldwide relations, exchange, and movement arrangements.

What's in store is a mind boggling embroidery woven with strings of development, difficulties, and valuable open doors. While these expectations give a brief look into what might lie ahead, it's memorable's essential that what's to come isn't permanently established. It is formed by our activities, choices, and flexibility.

In exploring the future, society should stay coordinated, open to change, and focused on resolving squeezing worldwide issues, from environmental change to monetary imbalance. By tackling the force of innovation, cultivating inclusivity, embracing maintainability, and maintaining moral standards, we can all in all control our reality toward a future that is more brilliant, more fair, and loaded up with guarantee. The excursion ahead is questionable, yet it is additionally a chance to shape the world we try to make for a long time into the future.

9.1 The Evolving Cloud Landscape in India

The distributed computing scene in India has been quickly developing lately, reflecting worldwide patterns in innovation reception and computerized change. As one of the world's quickest developing economies, India has seen a flood in cloud administrations usage across different areas. In this investigation, we will dive into the advancing cloud scene in India, featuring key patterns, difficulties, and valuable open doors that are forming the country's computerized future.

Quick Reception of Cloud Administrations

India's reception of cloud administrations has been out and out noteworthy. Organizations of all sizes, from new companies to huge undertakings, have embraced distributed computing as a way to upgrade readiness, versatility, and cost-productivity. The cloud has turned into the foundation of the advanced change venture for Indian organizations.

Computerized India Drive

The Indian government's Computerized India drive, sent off in 2015, plays had an essential impact in speeding up cloud reception. The program means to change India into a carefully enabled society and information economy. It has prodded interests in advanced framework, e-administration, and the utilization of cloud administrations to work on open administrations and government tasks.

Multi-Cloud and Crossover Cloud Procedures

As associations in India become progressively cloud-clever, they are embracing multi-cloud and crossover cloud systems. This approach permits organizations to use the qualities of various cloud suppliers while keeping up with command over delicate information. Organizations are utilizing a blend of public, private, and cross breed mists to streamline execution, versatility, and cost-viability.

Startup Biological system

India's dynamic startup environment has benefited colossally from cloud advances. Cloud administrations furnish new companies with the adaptability and adaptability expected to develop quickly without monstrous forthright foundation costs. Indian new businesses are upsetting different ventures, including internet business, fintech, healthtech, and edtech, on account of their cloud-controlled arrangements.

Edge Registering and IoT

The multiplication of Web of Things (IoT) gadgets and the interest for ongoing information handling have brought about edge registering arrangements in India. Edge registering carries handling power nearer to the information source, lessening inertness and further developing the general client experience. Businesses like assembling, agribusiness, and strategies are utilizing edge figuring to streamline activities.

Information Restriction and Consistence

Information confinement guidelines have been an unmistakable point in India's cloud scene. The public authority has acquainted measures with guarantee that specific classifications of delicate information are put away and handled inside the country. This has prompted cloud suppliers laying out server farms in India to consent to these guidelines while offering low-dormancy administrations to neighborhood clients.

Security and Consistence Difficulties

While cloud reception is on the ascent, worries about information security and consistence remain. Indian organizations are attempting to guarantee that their cloud arrangements stick to administrative necessities and industry norms. Information breaks and cyberattacks present critical dangers, provoking associations to put resources into hearty network safety measures and information insurance systems.

Abilities Lack

The developing interest for cloud mastery has made a lack of gifted experts in India. There is a requirement for more cloud modelers, designers, and security experts to help the sending and the board of cloud conditions. To overcome this issue, preparing and confirmation programs are acquiring prominence.

Computerized reasoning and AI

India is turning into a center for man-made brainpower (simulated intelligence) and AI (ML) development. Cloud stages offer the computational power and instruments essential for man-made intelligence and ML improvement. Organizations in medical services, money, and online business are utilizing man-made intelligence and ML to acquire bits of knowledge, upgrade client encounters, and drive business development.

Cloud-Local Turn of events

Cloud-local improvement works on, including containerization and microservices engineering, are building up some momentum in India. These methodologies empower the fast turn of events and sending of uses, making it more straightforward for associations to enhance and repeat. Kubernetes and compartment coordination are becoming standard apparatuses in the engineer tool stash.

E-Administration and Public Administrations

The Indian government has utilized cloud innovation to upgrade e-administration and convey public administrations all the more productively. Cloud-based stages empower residents to get to taxpayer driven organizations internet, decreasing desk work and regulatory deferrals. Drives like the Aadhaar computerized character framework and the Brought together Installments Point of interaction (UPI) have changed advanced admittance and monetary incorporation.

Future Possibilities

The cloud scene in India is ready for additional development and advancement. Key patterns to watch incorporate the extension of 5G organizations, the improvement of edge registering biological systems, the advancement of cloud-local innovations, and the continuous assembly of IoT, man-made intelligence, and cloud administrations.

The developing cloud scene in India is a demonstration of the country's obligation to computerized change and mechanical advancement. With quick reception of cloud benefits, a unique startup environment, government-driven drives, and a developing accentuation on information security and consistence, India is strategically situated to tackle the force of the cloud for financial development and social turn of events.

While difficulties, for example, abilities deficiencies and network safety dangers persevere, they are met earnestly and advancement. The eventual fate of the cloud in India vows to energize, with valuable open doors for organizations, business people, and the public authority to team up in building an all the more carefully comprehensive and prosperous country. As India proceeds with its groundbreaking process in the cloud time, it fills in as a convincing illustration of how innovation can drive positive change at both public and individual levels.

9.2 Emerging Technologies (Edge Computing, Quantum Computing)

In our consistently advancing mechanical scene, two noteworthy advancements have arisen as major advantages: Edge Processing and Quantum Registering. These advancements vow to change the manner in which we process and break down information, opening up additional opportunities in fields going from network protection to medical care. In this investigation, we will dive into the universe of arising advancements, zeroing in Nervous Figuring and Quantum Registering, to grasp their possible effect on our future.

1. **Edge Registering: Carrying Handling Nearer to the Source**
1. **The Fundamentals of Edge Registering**
   Edge Registering is a change in perspective by they way we handle

information handling and examination. Not at all like customary distributed computing, which unifies information handling in far off server farms, Edge Registering processes information nearer to the source, normally at or close to the edge of the organization. This empowers quicker reaction times, diminished inactivity, and further developed productivity.

2. **Use Cases and Applications**

1. **IoT and Brilliant Gadgets:** Edge Processing is imperative for the Web of Things (IoT). It permits savvy gadgets to deal with information locally, diminishing the requirement for consistent information transmission to focal servers. This is basic for applications like independent vehicles and shrewd urban communities.

2. **Continuous Examination:** Edge Processing empowers constant investigation for enterprises like assembling, medical services, and money. For instance, in assembling, sensors on apparatus can handle information locally to identify abnormalities or execution issues right away.

3. **Content Conveyance:** Content suppliers use edge servers to store and convey content nearer to clients. This diminishes content conveyance times and reduces network clog, bringing about a smoother client experience.

4. **Independent Frameworks:** Independent robots, robots, and vehicles depend Tense Registering for split-second direction. This innovation is crucial for wellbeing basic applications.

3. Advantages and Difficulties

1. **Decreased Inactivity:** Edge Figuring essentially lessens dormancy, making it ideal for applications where ongoing handling is vital.

2. **Transmission capacity Proficiency:** By handling information at the edge, Edge Registering lessens how much information that should be sent to focal servers, saving transfer speed and diminishing organization blockage.

3. **Protection and Security:** Information handling at the edge improves security and security. Touchy information can be handled locally, lessening the gamble of information breaks during transmission.

4. **Intricacy:** Carrying out Edge Registering can be mind boggling, as it requires conveying framework nearer to the edge gadgets. Also, overseeing dispersed frameworks can challenge.

II. Quantum Processing: Registering's Quantum Jump

1. **The Quantum Processing Transformation**
   Quantum Processing is an outlook changing innovation that use the standards of quantum mechanics to perform calculations that were beforehand outside the realm of possibilities for old style PCs. Rather than utilizing pieces, which can address either 0 or 1, quantum PCs use quantum bits or qubits, which can exist in various states all the while because of a peculiarity called superposition.

2. **Use Cases and Applications**

1. **Cryptography:** Quantum PCs can possibly break existing encryption techniques, presenting both a danger and an open door. Scientists are dealing with quantum-safe encryption strategies.

2. **Drug Revelation:** Quantum processing can reenact atomic collaborations with extraordinary exactness, essentially speeding up drug disclosure and advancement.

3. **Streamlining:** Quantum calculations can take care of intricate improvement issues quicker than traditional PCs. This has applications in coordinated factors, store network the executives, and money.

4. **AI:** Quantum registering can possibly upset AI by speeding up the preparation of perplexing models and further developing example acknowledgment.

3. Advantages and Difficulties

1. **Dramatic Speedup:** Quantum PCs can tackle specific issues dramatically quicker than traditional PCs, which is especially significant for complex logical and numerical reenactments.
2. **Quantum Matchless quality:** Accomplishing quantum matchless quality, where a quantum PC beats the most impressive traditional supercomputers, is a huge achievement in the field.
3. **Blunder Adjustment:** Quantum PCs are helpless to mistakes because of their aversion to ecological elements. Creating mistake revision strategies is a significant test.
4. **Cost and Adaptability:** Building and keeping up with quantum PCs is exorbitant, and they are not yet as versatile as old style PCs.

Edge Processing and Quantum Figuring address two particular however similarly extraordinary aspects of our innovative future. Edge Registering brings information handling nearer to the source, empowering ongoing navigation, diminishing idleness, and upgrading protection and security. It is the foundation of the Web of Things, fueling brilliant gadgets, independent frameworks, and continuous investigation. In any case, it additionally presents difficulties concerning intricacy and foundation the executives.

Then again, Quantum Figuring saddles the brain bowing properties of quantum mechanics to take care of issues that have baffled old style PCs for a really long time. Its applications range from cryptography and medication disclosure to streamlining and AI. However, quantum processing faces obstacles with regards to blunder adjustment, cost, and adaptability.

These arising advances are not only logical interests but rather amazing assets that will shape the eventual fate of enterprises, economies, and social orders. As we keep on investigating the potential and limits of Edge Registering and Quantum Figuring, joint effort between specialists, organizations, and state run administrations will be pivotal in conquering difficulties and bridling their maximum capacity. The excursion ahead vows to energize, as we open new wildernesses in innovation and extend the limits of what is conceivable in the computerized age.

9.3 Regulatory and Legislative Changes

In our quickly developing world, administrative and official changes assume a vital part in forming the manner in which social orders capability, organizations work, and people carry on with their lives.

From monetary guidelines to medical care approaches, natural regulations to information security, the scene of administration is in steady motion. In this investigation, we will dive into the effect of administrative and regulative changes and techniques for people, organizations, and legislatures to explore this unique landscape.

1. **The Effect of Administrative and Regulative Changes**

   Financial Ramifications

   Administrative changes have broad consequences for the economy. They can impact market elements, exchange arrangements, tax collection, and shopper conduct. For example, changes in charge regulations can affect corporate methodologies, speculation choices, and family funds. Essentially, exchange guidelines can impact global trade and supply chains.

   Industry-Explicit Effect

   Various enterprises are dependent upon a horde of guidelines that can significantly affect their tasks. In medical services, for instance, changes in medical services regulation can affect the conveyance of care, drug advancement, and protection inclusion. In the monetary area, administrative changes can influence loaning rehearses, risk the executives, and financial backer certainty.

   Development and Innovation

   Administrative and regulative changes can either encourage or prevent development and mechanical headways. Protected innovation regulations, information assurance guidelines, and patent arrangements can impact how organizations put resources into innovative work and safeguard their developments. In addition, strategies connected with arising advances like man-made consciousness, independent vehicles, and biotechnology are ceaselessly developing.

Natural Effect

Ecological guidelines are basic for tending to environmental change, contamination, and regular asset protection. Changes in natural regulation can drive interests in environmentally friendly power, impact corporate manageability methodologies, and shape protection endeavors.

Wellbeing and Security

Guidelines connected with wellbeing and security influence people on an individual level. Working environment security guidelines safeguard representatives, while food handling regulations guarantee the quality and wellbeing of consumables. General wellbeing approaches, as featured during the Coronavirus pandemic, are instrumental in defending public prosperity.

Information Protection and Security

In the advanced age, information protection and security guidelines have acquired tremendous significance.

Regulations like the European Association's Overall Information Assurance Guideline (GDPR) and the California Buyer Protection Act (CCPA) have set new principles for how organizations gather, store, and utilize individual information. Rebelliousness can bring about powerful fines and legitimate results.

Social and Social Effect

Regulative changes can have significant social and social ramifications. For instance, changes in marriage regulations, social equality regulation, and migration approaches can rethink cultural standards, advance inclusivity, and impact public talk.

2. **Methodologies for Exploring Administrative and Regulative Changes**

Remain Informed

The most vital phase in exploring administrative and official changes is to remain informed. People, organizations, and legislatures ought to lay out systems for checking improvements in applicable regions. Buying into industry pamphlets, taking part in proficient affiliations, and following media sources can give important bits of knowledge.

Take part in Backing

Organizations and associations can effectively take part in backing endeavors to impact strategy changes. This might include campaigning, joining industry affiliations, or partaking in open discussions. Backing can assist with molding strategies in manners that line up with an organization's objectives and values.

Consistence and Variation

For organizations, consistence with new guidelines is principal. This might require functional changes, interests in innovation and framework, and the advancement of new approaches and strategies. Routinely exploring and refreshing consistence measures is fundamental.

Risk The executives

Risk the executives techniques ought to be adjusted to represent administrative and authoritative changes. Organizations ought to lead risk appraisals to distinguish likely weaknesses and foster emergency courses of action to relieve any antagonistic impacts.

Legitimate Insight

Drawing in legitimate direction with aptitude in the important administrative regions can be instrumental in figuring out the ramifications of authoritative changes and guaranteeing consistence. Lawful counsel can assist organizations with exploring complex legitimate structures.

Expansion and Development

Organizations can proactively enhance their activities and put resources into development to adjust to evolving guidelines. For instance, enhancing product offerings or venturing into new business sectors can diminish dependence on a solitary administrative climate.

Public Commitment and Promotion

People can take part in broad daylight talk on official matters by casting a ballot, supporting associations that line up with their qualities, and drawing in with policymakers through letters, petitions, and promotion gatherings.

Schooling and Mindfulness

Bringing issues to light and instructing people in general about the ramifications of regulative changes can be an incredible asset. This can prompt informed direction and a more drawn in populace.

Joint effort and Discourse

Legislatures, organizations, and common society associations ought to take part in cooperative discourse to foster strategies that balance different interests. Open correspondence channels can prompt more compelling and evenhanded regulation.

Administrative and regulative changes are a basic piece of our developing society. While they can present difficulties and disturb laid out standards, they additionally give valuable open doors to positive change. Exploring this unique scene requires carefulness, flexibility, and proactive commitment.

By remaining educated, taking part in support, guaranteeing consistence, overseeing gambles, looking for legitimate advice, enhancing, and cultivating joint effort, people, organizations, and state run administrations can explore administrative and authoritative changes really. In doing as such, they can add to the improvement of arrangements that advance monetary development, shield individual privileges, safeguard the climate, and address the perplexing difficulties within recent memory. The way ahead might be dubious, however with educated and proactive endeavors, we can shape a future that mirrors our aggregate qualities and goals.

9.4 Preparing for the Future

What's to come is a domain of vulnerability, yet it is a landscape we as a whole should navigate. As people, organizations, and social orders, we are continually confronted with difficulties, potential open doors, and advancing scenes. While we can't anticipate each diversion out and about ahead, we can set ourselves up to explore the vulnerabilities representing things to come with strength and versatility. In this investigation, we will dig into systems for getting ready for the future, guaranteeing that we make due as well as flourish notwithstanding change.

1. **Embrace Deep rooted Learning**
The Significance of Long lasting Learning
Deep rooted learning is the foundation of getting ready for what's to come. In a quickly impacting world, obtaining new information and abilities is fundamental for individual and expert development. Consistently overhauling your abilities keeps you versatile and cutthroat in the gig market.
Online Instruction and Expertise Advancement
The computerized age has democratized instruction, with a plenty of online courses, instructional exercises, and assets accessible. Stages like Coursera, edX, and Khan Institute offer many courses, making it more straightforward than at any other time to procure new abilities and information.
Proficient Affirmations
Procuring proficient accreditations in your field can improve your capabilities and open up new profession valuable open doors. Numerous businesses have affirmation programs that approve your mastery and exhibit your obligation to progressing learning.

2. **Encourage Flexibility and Versatility**
Develop Versatility
Versatility is the capacity to quickly return from difficulty. Creating versatility includes developing mental and close to home fortitude, figuring out how to adapt to pressure, and fostering a positive mentality. Versatile people are better prepared to confront difficulties and difficulties.
Versatility Notwithstanding Change

Versatility is a key ability to survive in a universe of consistent change. Being available to groundbreaking thoughts, adaptable in your methodology, and ready to embrace change can assist you with flourishing in advancing conditions.

Stress The executives

Stress is a characteristic reaction to change and vulnerability. Figuring out how to oversee pressure through methods like contemplation, care, and exercise can upgrade your psychological and profound prosperity.

3. **Monetary Readiness**

Crisis Assets

Building a backup stash is vital for monetary strength. Having reserve funds put away for surprising costs or employment cutback gives a security net during testing times.

Contributing as long as possible

Contributing carefully can assist you with creating financial stability over the long haul. Enhance your ventures and spotlight on long haul objectives. Consider counseling a monetary consultant to go with informed speculation choices.

Monetary Proficiency

Understanding individual accounting is fundamental for settling on informed conclusions about saving, effective money management, and overseeing obligation. Monetary education courses and assets can assist you with acquiring a superior handle of your funds.

4. **Wellbeing and Health**

Focus on Wellbeing

Wellbeing is your most significant resource. Focus on physical, mental, and close to home prosperity by embracing a sound way of life. Customary activity, a reasonable eating regimen, and satisfactory rest are crucial.

Psychological well-being Mindfulness

Psychological well-being is pretty much as significant as actual wellbeing. Be proactive in overseeing pressure, uneasiness, and sorrow. Look for proficient assistance when required and decrease the disgrace related with emotional well-being issues.

Preventive Medical services

Standard check-ups and preventive medical services measures can distinguish and address medical problems early, diminishing the effect of future wellbeing challenges.

5. **Adjust to Mechanical Changes**

Remain Well informed

Innovation is continually advancing, and it is fundamental for keep awake to date. Find out more about arising advancements in your field, and be available to taking on new devices and stages.

Network protection Mindfulness

As innovation propels, so do network safety dangers. Safeguard your computerized resources by rehearsing great online protection cleanliness, utilizing solid passwords, and remaining informed about likely dangers.

6. **Natural Cognizance**

Maintainability Practices

Embrace maintainable living practices to lessen your ecological impression. Rationing assets, lessening waste, and supporting eco-accommodating drives add to a more reasonable future.

Environmental Change Mindfulness

Remain informed about environmental change and its effects. Support approaches and drives pointed toward moderating environmental change and safeguarding the climate.

7. **Fabricate Solid Connections**

Network and Interface

Assembling and keeping up serious areas of strength for with is fundamental for individual and expert development. Organizing gives open doors to coordinated effort, mentorship, and backing.

The capacity to understand people on a deeper level

Foster capacity to understand people on a deeper level to successfully explore connections. Understanding and dealing with your own feelings, as well as relating to other people, encourages good collaborations.

8. **Plan for Retirement**

Retirement Reserve funds

Plan for your retirement by consistently adding to retirement bank accounts, for example, 401(k)s or IRAs. Begin as soon as conceivable to exploit accumulate interest.

Retirement Way of life

Consider what sort of way of life you need in retirement and put forth monetary objectives likewise. Make a retirement plan that lines up with your goals.

Getting ready for what's in store isn't tied in with foreseeing everything about what lies ahead however about furnishing yourself with the abilities, attitude, and assets to flourish in a consistently impacting world. Embracing long lasting picking up, encouraging strength and versatility, focusing on monetary readiness, wellbeing, and health, adjusting to mechanical changes, embracing natural awareness, building solid connections, and anticipating retirement are techniques that engage you to explore the vulnerabilities representing things to come with certainty and flexibility.

By making proactive strides and being available to development and change, you can plan for the future as well as shape it in manners that line up with your qualities and yearnings. The excursion forward might be questionable, however with the right attitude and arrangement, you can embrace the difficulties and open doors that what's in store holds.

Chapter 10

Recommendations and Actionable Insights

In a quickly impacting world, the capacity to distil data, draw significant bits of knowledge, and form noteworthy suggestions is a basic expertise. Whether in business, strategy making, or individual navigation, the most common way of changing information into significant bits of knowledge is fundamental for going with informed decisions and driving achievement. In this thorough investigation, we will dig into the workmanship and study of suggestions and noteworthy experiences, looking at their importance, procedures, and genuine applications across different areas.

1. **Figuring out Suggestions and Significant Bits of knowledge**
   Proposals Characterized
   Proposals are direction, counsel, or ideas gave in view of examination, experience, or aptitude. They help people, associations, and leaders decide and make moves that line up with their targets and values.
   Noteworthy Experiences Characterized

Noteworthy experiences are explicit, information driven perceptions or discoveries that can be followed up on to accomplish wanted results. They are the aftereffect of top to bottom investigation of information, which might include distinguishing patterns, examples, or amazing open doors.

2. **The Meaning of Proposals and Significant Experiences**

Informed Navigation

Proposals and significant experiences engage people and associations to pursue informed choices. They give a make way forward, assisting with exploring complex circumstances and vulnerabilities.

Upper hand

In the business world, noteworthy bits of knowledge can prompt an upper hand. Associations that can bridle information to drive choices and activities are better situated to develop, advance cycles, and serve clients successfully.

Productivity and Viability

Suggestions and significant bits of knowledge advance proficiency by zeroing in endeavors on what makes the biggest difference. They assist with dispensing assets really, lessen squander, and smooth out activities.

Risk Alleviation

By recognizing likely dangers and open doors, suggestions and bits of knowledge empower proactive gamble relief. Leaders can make preventive moves or foster alternate courses of action.

3. **Approaches for Creating Suggestions and Significant Bits of knowledge**

Information Assortment and Handling

The most important phase in creating experiences is information assortment. This might include gathering information from different sources, including overviews, sensors, online entertainment, or deals. Information is then handled and cleaned to guarantee exactness and pertinence.

Information Investigation and Representation

Information investigation strategies, for example, factual examination, AI, and information mining, are utilized to uncover examples, patterns, and relationships inside the information. Perception apparatuses like diagrams and charts assist with introducing complex information in a reasonable organization.

Contextualization

Understanding the setting of the information is urgent. Contextualization includes considering variables like timing, area, and outer impacts that might influence the translation of information.

Interdisciplinary Joint effort

Producing suggestions and experiences frequently requires interdisciplinary coordinated effort. Specialists from various fields, like information science, brain research, financial matters, and designing, may team up to acquire a comprehensive point of view.

4. True Applications

Business and Advertising

In the business world, suggestions and significant bits of knowledge drive showcasing systems, item advancement, and client commitment. Models remember customized item proposals for internet business sites and information driven promoting efforts.

Medical services and Medication

Medical services suppliers utilize significant experiences to work on persistent results and enhance asset portion. Prescient examination can assist emergency clinics with expecting patient affirmation rates, while accuracy medication depends on experiences from genomics information.

Money and Speculation

Monetary establishments depend on significant bits of knowledge to oversee chances, distinguish fake exercises, and settle on venture choices. Quantitative examination and algorithmic exchanging are instances of bits of knowledge driven rehearses finance.

Public Approach and Administration

States use bits of knowledge to illuminate public strategy choices. Information on socioeconomics, training, and medical care results assist with molding approaches connected with schooling, social government assistance, and general wellbeing.

Ecological Preservation

Preservation associations utilize significant bits of knowledge to safeguard environments and untamed life. Bits of knowledge from remote detecting information, for instance, assist with checking deforestation and plan protection endeavors.

Innovation and Development

In the innovation area, suggestions drive client encounters and programming advancement. Calculations that suggest content, items, or associations are implanted in online entertainment stages and web based business sites.

5. ## Difficulties and Contemplations

Information Quality and Protection

Guaranteeing the quality and protection of information used to create suggestions and experiences is vital. Unfortunate information quality can prompt wrong ends, while information breaks can think twice about.

Inclination and Reasonableness

Proposals and bits of knowledge can be affected by predisposition in information assortment or calculation plan. Endeavors should be made to recognize and relieve inclination to guarantee fair and evenhanded results.

Moral Contemplations

The moral ramifications of suggestions and experiences ought to be painstakingly thought of. Choices in light of experiences might affect people, networks, and society at large, making moral rules fundamental.

Interpretability

Complex calculations can produce bits of knowledge that are hard to decipher. Guaranteeing that leaders can comprehend and believe the bits of knowledge is basic for compelling execution.

6. **Procedures for Compelling Execution**

Characterize Clear Goals

Obviously characterize the targets and objectives you plan to accomplish through proposals and significant bits of knowledge. This gives a reasonable course to the examination cycle.

Select Proper Instruments and Innovations

Pick the right devices and advancements for information assortment, investigation, and representation. Consider factors like information volume, intricacy, and the particular area of utilization.

Construct Cross-Useful Groups

Gather cross-useful groups with assorted ability to handle complex issues. Coordinated effort between information researchers, area specialists, and leaders upgrades the nature of bits of knowledge.

Consistently Screen and Update

Suggestions and bits of knowledge might advance after some time as new information opens up or conditions change. Consistently screen and update your proposals to guarantee their importance.

Criticism Circles

Lay out criticism circles that take into consideration consistent improvement. Gather criticism from clients or partners to refine suggestions and make them more viable.

Straightforwardness and Correspondence

Keep up with straightforwardness in the dynamic cycle and impart discoveries obviously. This encourages trust and guarantees that suggestions are generally welcomed.

7. **The Job of Man-made brainpower (artificial intelligence)**

Artificial intelligence Driven Suggestions

Man-made brainpower assumes a huge part in creating proposals and bits of knowledge. AI calculations can investigate immense datasets and adjust proposals in light of client conduct and inclinations.

Challenges and Moral Contemplations

Artificial intelligence driven proposals likewise raise difficulties connected with predisposition, decency, and protection. Guaranteeing that computer based intelligence frameworks are intended to moderate inclination and safeguard client security is essential.

8. The Eventual fate of Suggestions and Significant Bits of knowledge

Headways in simulated intelligence and AI

As man-made intelligence and AI innovations keep on propelling, proposals and bits of knowledge will turn out to be considerably more exact and customized. This will affect different areas, including medical care, online business, and amusement.

Moral artificial intelligence and Guideline

The improvement of moral artificial intelligence and administrative structures will be a concentration later on. State run administrations and associations should address moral worries connected with artificial intelligence driven suggestions.

Cross-Space Bits of knowledge

Cross-space bits of knowledge that consolidate information from different sources and enterprises will turn out to be progressively significant. These bits of knowledge can drive development and illuminate all encompassing navigation.

Suggestions and noteworthy bits of knowledge are useful assets for pursuing informed choices and driving accomplishment across different spaces. Whether in business, medical care, finance, public approach, or innovation, the capacity to change information into noteworthy direction is fundamental in an undeniably mind boggling and information rich world.

To tackle the maximum capacity of proposals and bits of knowledge, people, associations, and policymakers should address difficulties connected with information quality, predisposition, morals, and straightforwardness. By executing viable methodologies, cultivating interdisciplinary joint effort, and embracing mechanical headways, we can explore the developing scene of suggestions and bits of knowledge to make a future that is educated, fair, and driven by information driven independent direction.

10.1 Developing a Cloud-First Roadmap

In the steadily developing scene of data innovation, embracing a cloud-first procedure has turned into a foundation of present day computerized change. Distributed computing offers versatility, adaptability, cost-proficiency, and dexterity, settling on it a convincing decision for associations trying to enhance and flourish in the present serious climate. In this investigation, we will dig into the most common way of fostering a cloud-first guide, featuring key contemplations, advantages, difficulties, and best practices for associations leaving on this groundbreaking excursion.

1. **Understanding the Cloud-First Methodology**

   What is a Cloud-First Technique?

   A cloud-first technique is a methodology where associations focus on cloud-based arrangements and administrations for their IT framework and application needs. It includes taking on an outlook that favors cloud administrations over conventional on-premises arrangements.

   Why Go Cloud-First?

   Adaptability: Associations can without much of a stretch scale assets up or down in light of interest.

   Cost-Effectiveness: Pay-more only as costs arise evaluating models assist with controlling expenses.

   Adaptability: Cloud administrations empower remote work, adaptability, and openness.

   Development: Cloud-based apparatuses and advances cultivate advancement and spryness.

Security: Cloud suppliers put vigorously in safety efforts, improving generally speaking online protection.

2. **Fostering a Cloud-First Guide**

Appraisal of Present status

Prior to setting out on a cloud-first excursion, associations ought to survey their ongoing IT foundation, applications, and business processes. This appraisal recognizes regions where cloud arrangements can bring the most worth.

Characterizing Targets and Objectives

Obviously characterize the targets and objectives that the cloud-first technique plans to accomplish. These goals can incorporate expense reserve funds, further developed adaptability, upgraded cooperation, or quicker time-to-advertise for new items and administrations.

Choosing Cloud Administration Models

Foundation as a Help (IaaS): Gives virtualized registering assets.

Stage as a Help (PaaS): Offers a stage and instruments for application improvement.

Programming as a Help (SaaS): Conveys programming applications over the web.

Choosing Cloud Sending Models

Public Cloud: Administrations are facilitated by third-get-together suppliers and available over the web.

Confidential Cloud: Administrations are facilitated on a devoted foundation, offering more control and security.

Half breed Cloud: A blend of public and confidential mists, permitting information and applications to be divided among them.

Cost Investigation and Planning

Direct an expense investigation to gauge the costs related with the cloud-first system. Foster a spending plan that considers movement costs, progressing functional costs, and possible investment funds.

Security and Consistence

Address security and consistence necessities. Carry out powerful safety efforts and guarantee that cloud suppliers stick to vital consistence principles, particularly in profoundly managed ventures.

Information Movement and Reconciliation

Plan for the movement of existing information and applications to the cloud. Guarantee that information reconciliation with on-premises frameworks and other cloud administrations is consistent.

Staff Preparing and Expertise Improvement

Give preparing and ability improvement open doors for IT staff to furnish them with the fundamental information and aptitude to oversee cloud-based framework really.

Pilot Undertakings and Evidence of Idea

Before a full-scale movement, lead pilot tasks or confirmation of idea (PoC) drives to test cloud administrations, assess their presentation, and recognize any possible difficulties.

Movement Methodology

Foster a relocation technique that frames the succession of movement, conditions, and rollback plans in the event of issues. Consider a staged way to deal with limit interruptions.

3. **Advantages of a Cloud-First System**

Cost Investment funds

Cloud administrations offer expense investment funds through decreased capital costs (CapEx) and pay-more only as costs arise models. Associations can keep away from the forthright expenses of equipment and server farms.

Versatility

Cloud assets can be increased or down to satisfy fluctuating need. This adaptability is particularly important for organizations with occasional or variable responsibilities.

Worldwide Reach

Cloud suppliers offer a worldwide organization of server farms, empowering associations to extend their scope and serve clients overall without huge framework speculations.

Quicker Time-to-Market

Cloud-based advancement instruments and stages work with quick application improvement and sending, decreasing chance to-advertise for new items and administrations.

Business Congruity and Calamity Recuperation

Cloud suppliers offer strong reinforcement and calamity recuperation arrangements, guaranteeing information strength and limiting margin time if there should arise an occurrence of interruptions.

Coordinated effort and Remote Work

Cloud-based coordinated effort apparatuses and remote work capacities empower representatives to work from anyplace, advancing efficiency and adaptability.

4. Difficulties and Contemplations

Information Security and Protection

Safeguarding delicate information in the cloud is a top concern. Associations should execute strong safety efforts and guarantee consistence with information insurance guidelines.

Merchant Lock-In

Contingent vigorously upon a solitary cloud supplier can prompt merchant secure. To moderate this gamble, consider multi-cloud or cross breed cloud methodologies.

Execution and Inertness

Execution issues and dormancy can happen, particularly for applications that require low-idleness admittance to information. Choosing the right cloud supplier and area is fundamental.

Cost Administration

While cloud administrations offer expense investment funds, associations should screen and deal with their cloud spending to stay away from unforeseen costs.

Abilities Hole

A deficiency of cloud skill can present difficulties. Associations ought to put resources into preparing and expertise advancement for their IT groups.

5. **Best Practices for a Fruitful Cloud-First Methodology**

Persistent Observing and Enhancement

Routinely screen cloud assets, utilization, and expenses. Enhance asset designation to amplify cost-proficiency.

Information Reinforcement and Recuperation

Carry out hearty information reinforcement and recuperation techniques to guarantee information uprightness and business coherence.

Consistence and Administration

Lay out clear administration approaches to guarantee consistence with industry guidelines and interior principles.

Joint effort and Correspondence

Cultivate cooperation and correspondence among IT and specialty units to adjust cloud techniques to authoritative objectives.

Standard Security Reviews

Direct normal security reviews and infiltration testing to distinguish weaknesses and reinforce safety efforts.

Half and half and Multi-Cloud Approaches

Think about half and half or multi-cloud procedures to keep away from merchant secure and upgrade adaptability.

Advancing Design

Configuration cloud models that can develop and adjust to changing business necessities and mechanical headways.

Fostering a cloud-first guide is an essential basic for associations looking to bridle the groundbreaking force of distributed computing. Via cautiously surveying present status, setting clear goals, choosing the right cloud administration and arrangement models, and tending to security and consistence contemplations, associations can effectively explore the computerized change venture.

The advantages of a cloud-first system, including cost reserve funds, versatility, worldwide reach, and business progression, are convincing.

Nonetheless, associations should likewise address difficulties connected with information security, seller secure in, execution, cost administration, and abilities improvement. By sticking to best practices and persistently checking and streamlining cloud assets, associations can open the maximum capacity of the cloud and drive development, proficiency, and seriousness in the computerized age.

10.2 Building a Business Case for Cloud Adoption

In the present computerized period, distributed computing has arisen as an extraordinary power that engages organizations to scale, enhance, and remain serious. Building a convincing business case for cloud reception is fundamental for associations looking to saddle the advantages of this innovation. In this investigation, we will dig into the most common way of making a vigorous business case for cloud reception, zeroing in on the key contemplations, benefits, difficulties, and best practices that can assist associations with pursuing informed choices.

1. **Grasping Cloud Reception**

   What is Cloud Reception?

   Cloud reception alludes to the most common way of progressing an association's IT foundation, applications, and administrations from on-premises server farms to cloud-based stages. It includes using distributed computing assets to store, make due, and convey information and applications.

   Why Embrace the Cloud?

   Adaptability: The capacity to increase assets or down in view of interest.

   Cost-Proficiency: Scaled down capital costs (CapEx) and pay-more only as costs arise estimating models.

   Adaptability and Dexterity: Speedy provisioning of assets for development and trial and error.

   Worldwide Come to: The capacity to serve clients and grow activities around the world.

Business Coherence: Vigorous debacle recuperation and reinforcement arrangements.

2. **Building a Business Case for Cloud Reception**

Evaluation of Present status

Start by evaluating the association's ongoing IT foundation, including equipment, programming, and server farm costs. Figure out the limits and limitations of the current framework.

Characterize Targets and Objectives

Obviously characterize the targets and objectives that cloud reception means to accomplish. Shared objectives incorporate expense investment funds, further developed adaptability, improved deftness, and quicker time-to-advertise.

Choosing the Right Cloud Administration Models

Foundation as a Help (IaaS): Gives virtualized figuring assets.

Stage as a Help (PaaS): Offers a stage and instruments for application improvement.

Programming as a Help (SaaS): Conveys programming applications over the web.

Choosing the Fitting Cloud Organization Models

Public Cloud: Administrations are facilitated by third-gathering suppliers and available over the web.

Confidential Cloud: Administrations are facilitated on a committed foundation, offering more control and security.

Crossover Cloud: A blend of public and confidential mists, permitting information and applications to be divided among them.

Cost Examination and Planning

Lead a careful expense investigation that gauges the costs related with cloud reception. Foster a financial plan that considers movement costs, progressing functional costs, and expected investment funds.

Security and Consistence

Address security and consistence necessities all along. Carry out hearty safety efforts and guarantee that cloud suppliers stick to essential consistence guidelines.

Information Movement and Incorporation

Plan for the movement of existing information and applications to the cloud. Guarantee that information combination with on-premises frameworks and other cloud administrations is consistent.

Staff Preparing and Expertise Advancement

Give preparing and ability improvement potential open doors for IT staff to outfit them with the vital information and aptitude to oversee cloud-based framework really.

Pilot Tasks and Evidence of Idea (PoC)

Before a full-scale relocation, lead pilot projects or PoC drives to test cloud administrations, assess their presentation, and recognize any expected difficulties.

Relocation System

Foster a relocation system that frames the grouping of movement, conditions, and rollback plans in the event of issues. Consider a staged way to deal with limit disturbances.

3. ### Advantages of Cloud Reception

Cost Investment funds

Cloud reception offers massive expense investment funds through scaled down CapEx, pay-more only as costs arise evaluating models, and proficient asset use.

Adaptability

Associations can undoubtedly increase cloud assets or down to fulfill fluctuating need, enhancing asset assignment and expenses.

Adaptability and Spryness

Cloud administrations give the spryness to rapidly arrangement assets, explore different avenues regarding new arrangements, and adjust to changing business needs.

Worldwide Reach

Cloud suppliers offer a worldwide organization of server farms, empowering associations to grow their span and serve clients overall without huge foundation ventures.

Business Congruity and Calamity Recuperation

Cloud suppliers offer strong reinforcement and calamity recuperation arrangements, guaranteeing information versatility and limiting personal time in the event of disturbances.

Joint effort and Remote Work

Cloud-based joint effort instruments and remote work abilities empower representatives to work from anyplace, advancing efficiency and adaptability.

4. **Difficulties and Contemplations**

   Information Security and Protection

   Safeguarding touchy information in the cloud is a top concern. Associations should carry out strong safety efforts and guarantee consistence with information insurance guidelines.

   Seller Lock-In

   Contingent vigorously upon a solitary cloud supplier can prompt seller secure. To relieve this gamble, consider multi-cloud or half and half cloud systems.

   Execution and Inertness

   Execution issues and inertness can happen, particularly for applications that require low-dormancy admittance to information. Choosing the right cloud supplier and area is fundamental.

   Cost Administration

   While cloud administrations offer expense reserve funds, associations should screen and deal with their cloud spending to stay away from surprising costs.

   Abilities Hole

   A lack of cloud skill can present difficulties. Associations ought to put resources into preparing and ability advancement for their IT groups.

5. **Best Practices for a Fruitful Cloud Reception**

Consistent Checking and Streamlining

Consistently screen cloud assets, use, and expenses. Improve asset portion to augment cost-proficiency.

Information Reinforcement and Recuperation

Execute hearty information reinforcement and recuperation systems to guarantee information trustworthiness and business progression.

Consistence and Administration

Lay out clear administration strategies to guarantee consistence with industry guidelines and inward norms.

Coordinated effort and Correspondence

Encourage cooperation and correspondence among IT and specialty units to adjust cloud systems to authoritative objectives.

Standard Security Reviews

Direct standard security reviews and entrance testing to recognize weaknesses and reinforce safety efforts.

Cross breed and Multi-Cloud Approaches

Think about cross breed or multi-cloud procedures to stay away from merchant secure and upgrade adaptability.

Developing Design

Configuration cloud structures that can develop and adjust to changing business prerequisites and innovative progressions.

Building a business case for cloud reception is an essential basic for associations looking to saddle the groundbreaking force of distributed computing. Via cautiously surveying the present status, characterizing targets and objectives, choosing the right cloud administration and sending models, and tending to security and consistence contemplations, associations can effectively explore the advanced change venture.

The advantages of cloud reception, including cost investment funds, adaptability, worldwide reach, and business progression, are convincing. Notwithstanding, associations should likewise address difficulties connected with information security, seller secure in, execution, cost administration, and abilities improvement. By sticking to best practices and ceaselessly checking and enhancing cloud assets, associations can open the maximum capacity of the cloud and drive advancement, proficiency, and seriousness in the computerized age.

10.3 Steps to Ensure Data Security and Compliance

Information is the backbone of current associations, and shielding it against dangers and it is vital to guarantee consistence with guidelines. Information security and consistence are fundamental for safeguarding touchy data as well as for keeping up with entrust with clients and partners. In this extensive investigation, we will dive into the basic advances that associations ought to take to guarantee information security and consistence, underscoring the significance of a proactive and comprehensive methodology.

1. **Figuring out Information Security and Consistence**
   Information Security Characterized
   Information security includes shielding information from unapproved access, exposure, change, or obliteration. It envelops different measures and techniques to shield information resources.
   Information Consistence Characterized
   Information consistence alludes to the adherence to administrative prerequisites and industry principles overseeing the assortment, stockpiling, handling, and treatment of information. Consistence guarantees that associations work inside legitimate and moral limits.

2. **The Meaning of Information Security and Consistence**
   Security of Delicate Data
   Information security shields touchy data, including client information, protected innovation, and monetary records, from breaks and cyberattacks.
   Trust and Notoriety
   Keeping up major areas of strength for with security rehearses constructs entrust with clients and partners. Information breaks can dissolve trust and harm an association's standing.
   Lawful and Monetary Results

Resistance with information security guidelines can bring about extreme lawful and monetary outcomes, including fines and prosecution.

Functional Congruity

Hearty information security and consistence measures guarantee functional coherence by limiting disturbances brought about by information breaks or administrative infringement.

3. **Moves toward Guarantee Information Security and Consistence**

Information Grouping and Stock

Start by ordering information in light of its responsiveness and significance. Make a stock that records where information dwells, who gets to it, and the way things are handled.

Risk Evaluation

Direct an exhaustive gamble evaluation to distinguish likely dangers and weaknesses. Survey the effect and probability of these dangers and focus on them in view of their seriousness.

Information Encryption

Scramble delicate information both on the way and very still. Encryption guarantees that regardless of whether information is compromised, it stays disjointed without the encryption keys.

Access Control

Carry out severe access controls to restrict information admittance to approved faculty as it were. Use job based admittance control (RBAC) and two-factor validation (2FA) to upgrade security.

Standard Security Reviews and Testing

Direct customary security reviews and weakness evaluations to distinguish shortcomings in your frameworks and applications. Perform infiltration testing to reproduce cyberattacks.

Information Reinforcements and Recuperation

Lay out hearty information reinforcement and recuperation methodology to guarantee information can be reestablished in case of information misfortune or a digital occurrence.

Security Mindfulness Preparing

Train workers on security best practices and teach them about the dangers of phishing assaults, social designing, and other security dangers.

Episode Reaction Plan

Foster an obvious occurrence reaction plan that frameworks moves toward take in case of a security episode. This plan ought to incorporate correspondence conventions and acceleration methods.

Information Protection Consistence

Comprehend and follow information insurance guidelines like GDPR, HIPAA, CCPA, or industry-explicit norms. Designate an Information Insurance Official (DPO) whenever required.

Information Minimization and Maintenance Approaches

Carry out information minimization rehearses by gathering and putting away just the information essential for business purposes. Lay out information maintenance approaches to oversee information lifecycle.

Seller and Outsider Gamble The board

Evaluate and screen the security practices of outsider sellers and specialist organizations who approach your information. Guarantee they meet your security and consistence prerequisites.

Standard Security Updates and Fix The board

Keep programming, working frameworks, and applications fully informed regarding security fixes and updates to address weaknesses.

Information Move Security

Execute secure conventions and encryption instruments while moving information between frameworks or to outer gatherings.

Secure Improvement Practices

Integrate security into the product improvement lifecycle

(SDLC). Direct code audits, static examination, and weakness checking.

4. **Best Practices for Guaranteeing Information Security and Consistence**

Nonstop Observing and Inspecting

Ceaselessly screen and review your frameworks and organizations for any unapproved access or information breaks. Robotized checking instruments can assist with identifying oddities.

Archive Strategies and Methodology

Archive all information security and consistence strategies and methodology. Guarantee that workers have simple admittance to these archives for reference.

Normal Representative Preparation

Give continuous preparation to representatives to keep them informed about the most recent security dangers and best practices. Support a security-cognizant culture.

Episode Reaction Drills

Lead ordinary occurrence reaction drills to test the adequacy of your reaction plan. Distinguish regions for development and update the arrangement appropriately.

Information Security Effect Appraisals (DPIA)

Lead DPIAs to survey and moderate the protection gambles related with information handling exercises. DPIAs are especially significant under GDPR.

Legitimate and Consistence Group Joint effort

Cultivate joint effort among IT and legitimate/consistence groups to guarantee that information safety efforts line up with lawful prerequisites and industry guidelines.

5. **Innovation Answers for Information Security and Consistence**

Information Misfortune Avoidance (DLP) Apparatuses

DLP arrangements help screen and forestall the unapproved sharing or spillage of touchy information.

Character and Access The board (IAM) Frameworks

IAM frameworks control and oversee client admittance to information and assets, guaranteeing that main approved clients approach.

Security Data and Occasion The board (SIEM) Frameworks

SIEM apparatuses gather and break down information from different sources to recognize and answer security episodes.

Encryption Innovations

Carry out encryption for information very still and on the way, utilizing solid encryption calculations and key administration rehearses.

Security Mechanization and Organization

Mechanize security cycles and reactions to address security dangers and episodes quickly.

Guaranteeing information security and consistence is a complex and progressing exertion that requests carefulness and responsibility from associations. By following the means and best practices framed in this investigation, associations can establish a safe and consistent climate for their information resources.

Information security and consistence are not simply specialized matters; they are basic parts of an association's standing, dependability, and legitimate standing. Associations that put resources into hearty information security and consistence measures safeguard their computerized resources as well as construct an establishment for long haul progress in an undeniably information driven world.

10.4 Nurturing a Cloud-Centric Culture

In the quickly advancing scene of innovation, associations are progressively perceiving the groundbreaking capability of distributed computing. Embracing cloud-driven culture isn't only about taking on new innovation; it addresses a crucial change in how associations work, develop, and contend in the computerized age. In this extensive investigation, we will dive into the idea of supporting a cloud-driven culture, why it is significant, and the procedures and best practices that associations can utilize to successfully cultivate this culture.

1. ## The Quintessence of a Cloud-Driven Culture
   ### Characterizing a Cloud-Driven Culture
   A cloud-driven culture is a hierarchical mentality that spots distributed computing at the center of its tasks, procedures, and dynamic cycles. It includes a bunch of values, ways of behaving, and rehearses that focus on the utilization of cloud assets for development and productivity.
   ### The Change in Outlook
   Moving to a cloud-driven culture includes a change in outlook from customary on-premises framework to embracing the cloud's versatility, dexterity, and extraordinary potential.

2. ## The Meaning of a Cloud-Driven Culture
   ### Advancement and Deftness
   A cloud-driven culture enables associations to enhance quickly, try different things with new arrangements, and adjust to changing business scenes. Cloud assets empower the speedy provisioning of foundation and administrations, cultivating nimbleness.
   ### Cost Effectiveness
   By utilizing cloud assets, associations can improve costs, decrease capital costs, and scale assets in light of interest. This cost-productivity is especially important for organizations with variable responsibilities.
   ### Worldwide Reach
   Cloud suppliers offer a worldwide organization of server farms, permitting associations to grow their scope and serve clients overall without huge foundation speculations.
   ### Security and Strength
   Cloud suppliers put vigorously in safety efforts and proposition powerful reinforcement and calamity recuperation arrangements. A cloud-driven culture can improve an association's security

stance and information flexibility.

Ability Fascination and Maintenance

Embracing current cloud advances can make an association more appealing to top ability, particularly among more youthful ages who are knowledgeable in cloud stages and devices.

3. **Procedures for Supporting a Cloud-Driven Culture**

Administration Purchase In and Backing

Initiative assumes a vital part in encouraging a cloud-driven culture. Pioneers should advocate cloud drives, set a model, and assign assets to help the progress.

Instruction and Preparing

Put resources into cloud instruction and preparing programs for representatives at all levels. Guarantee that staff have the information and abilities expected to actually use cloud assets.

Cross-Useful Joint effort

Cultivate joint effort among various offices, including IT, tasks, promoting, and finance. A cross-utilitarian methodology guarantees that cloud reception lines up with hierarchical objectives.

Advance a Culture of Trial and error

Urge workers to explore different avenues regarding new cloud advancements and arrangements. Establish a climate where disappointment is viewed as a chance for learning and improvement.

Clear Correspondence

Impart the advantages and goals of cloud reception straightforwardly. Guarantee that all partners comprehend the job of the cloud in accomplishing authoritative objectives.

Put forth Clear Objectives and Measurements

Characterize clear objectives and Key Execution Pointers (KPIs) for cloud reception drives. Consistently evaluate progress and change methodologies on a case by case basis.

Engage Workers

Engage workers to take responsibility for cloud-related projects. Support independence and obligation in direction.

Perceive and Reward Development

Perceive and remunerate representatives who add to cloud-driven drives and inventive arrangements. Affirmation can spur further advancement.

4. **Best Practices for Sustaining a Cloud-Driven Culture**

Embrace Cloud Local Advances

Embrace cloud-local advances and practices, like compartments and microservices, to use cloud capacities and construct versatile, strong applications completely.

Carry out DevOps Practices

Carry out DevOps rehearses that empower coordinated effort among improvement and activities groups. Robotization, persistent joining, and nonstop conveyance (CI/Cd) pipelines upgrade deftness.

Cloud Administration and Consistence

Lay out clear cloud administration arrangements to guarantee consistence with guidelines and cost control. Apparatuses and structures can assist with overseeing cloud assets actually.

Security by Plan

Execute safety efforts from the beginning of cloud projects. A culture of safety mindfulness and adherence to best practices is essential.

Information The board and Administration

Foster information the board and administration procedures to guarantee information uprightness, openness, and security in a cloud climate.

Standard Assessment and Enhancement

Consistently assess cloud assets and expenses. Advance asset allotment to expand cost-proficiency and execution.

Criticism Circles

Lay out criticism circles that permit representatives to give info and ideas to further developing cloud reception cycles and practices.

5. Defeating Difficulties

Protection from Change

Protection from change is quite difficult while sustaining a cloud-driven culture. Pioneers ought to address concerns and offer help for representatives adjusting to better approaches for working.

Abilities Hole

An abilities hole might exist inside the association. Put resources into preparing and ability improvement projects to overcome this issue and guarantee that representatives are capable in cloud advances.

Coordination with Heritage Frameworks

Coordinating cloud advancements with inheritance frameworks can be mind boggling. Foster movement procedures and consider mixture cloud ways to deal with overcome any barrier.

Security Concerns

Security is a top worry in a cloud-driven culture. Guarantee that strong safety efforts and consistence structures are set up to moderate dangers.

Supporting a cloud-driven culture is certainly not a one-time exertion yet a continuous excursion that requires responsibility, initiative, and a commitment to embracing change. Associations that effectively progress to a cloud-driven culture stand to acquire critical benefits regarding development, readiness, cost productivity, and security.

By executing the procedures and best practices illustrated in this investigation, associations can cultivate a culture that completely use the extraordinary force of distributed computing. In the computerized age, a cloud-driven culture isn't simply a decision; it is an essential basic for remaining serious and future-prepared.

www.ingramcontent.com/pod-product-compliance
Lightning Source LLC
LaVergne TN
LVHW022111210726
843510LV00015BA/1144